A PLACE
CALLED
GRACE

A MEMOIR

To Julie,
Best wishes!
Alison Rand

ALISON RAND

ISBN: 978-1-64184-027-9 (paperback)
ISBN: 978-1-64184-028-6 (ebook)

Della Vita Publishing
New York, NY USA

For David and Grace.

AUTHOR'S NOTE

In writing Part Two, which takes place in Rome, Italy, I relied on re-reading my three years of personal diaries, allowing me to enhance my memories of this important time in my life. In addition, some of the names have been changed to allow for confidentiality, but under no circumstances were the events or the people not true or part of my Rome experience. My time living in Italy has remained a significant aspect of my life, and I valued each and every person that came my way and with whom I had a friendship.

PROLOGUE

Though we travel the world over to find the beautiful, we must carry it with us or we find it not.

—Ralph Waldo Emerson

A third of my life ago I flew away.

I moved alone to a foreign country where I didn't have a job lined up, didn't speak the language well, and knew not a single person.

Some people said it was a brave thing to do. Others thought it was unwise, bordering on insane. Why would I leave a perfectly good life as an actress in New York? Why would I give up a hard-to-get Manhattan apartment with a (partial) view of the Hudson?

It was neither brave nor crazy. What even my friends did not realize was how desperate I felt, how lost.

I arrived in Rome without any particular direction. All I had was a goal and a fierce determination to try and change my life, to begin again where no one knew me. In the Eternal City, I hoped to find something lasting—a sense of permanence, a sense of belonging.

A home.

PART I

PART 1

1

1994

I t was always the same dream: I was swimming along in calm waters near the shoreline, doing the crawl, kicking evenly, my arms pulling me along. Gradually, I found I was swimming against the tide. I wasn't going anywhere. I had to kick harder, increase the power of my stroke. Soon even that wouldn't be enough, and I'd be swept out to sea.

I woke up in a cold sweat. Again. The clock said 4:13 a.m.

I stayed under the covers, steadying my breathing until sunrise. Then I stumbled to the kitchen and made myself a cup of coffee that I would sip, as I did every morning, in one of the comfortable bedroom chairs. From there I could gaze out the window. If I focused on a tiny space between two tall buildings that otherwise blocked my view, I could make out the smallest snippet of the Hudson River, and that calmed me.

I told myself again how fortunate I was. After all, I had what others believed was a satisfying life. At 37, I had abs that were just this side of washboard. I had the comfort of some good friends. Although struggling as an actress, I had my own place in Manhattan, which is no small thing.

Nevertheless, like my semi-view window, something in my life was blocked.

Every day was the same, right down to what I ate, and how I ate it. I measured it out—one glass of white wine and two cigarettes at 6:00 p.m. One spoonful of low-fat Ben & Jerry's at night before bed. I had become a careful eater ever since my short-lived career as a flight attendant, where I lived in fear of the monthly weigh-ins: One cup of whole-grain cereal with low-fat milk for breakfast, along with one and a half cups of super-strong coffee. Chicken salad on whole wheat with lettuce, tomato, and pickle for lunch.

I went to the gym five times a week in a short spandex top to show off my abs and form-fitted sweatpants to disguise my thighs, and always did the same routine: stationary bike for half an hour, strength training with five-pound weights, and a series of stretches. For a short time after those workouts, I was at peace until the endorphins subsided and I was once again adrift in a life that looked great from the outside, but felt lonely on the inside.

That morning as I nursed my one-and-a-half coffees, Denise called as she always did, at 9:30 a.m. like clockwork.

"Hey, honey," she said. "How was the date?" Denise, a Pat Benatar lookalike with a small, perfect nose and large almond-shaped brown eyes, worked in finance and was always buzzing with energy.

"The same, kind of boring," I said with a sigh.

"Hold on. I've got another call." A minute later, she was back. "Sorry, business," she apologized. "Honey, you sound so sad. What can I do?"

"I don't know," I said. "It's like I'm programmed to go through specific motions every day but without any purpose. I feel like a Stepford Wife. And I'm not even married!"

"How can you say that? You've got a body to die for, and you lead a glamorous life, surrounded by interesting people. I wish I had your life. I mean, look at you! You're an actress!"

"I *audition*," I corrected her. "That's different from having steady acting work."

I'd been the girl on the box and in the infomercial for Perfect Smile, a tooth-whitening paste. The producers praised me for my work on the TV ad for The Patch, a weight-control product that was being marketed across Europe. Whenever I was chosen for a commercial out of a field of 100 contenders, I felt special, singled out. It gave me a rush and made me feelthink I had been right to choose a career in acting. I wasn't aiming to be Meryl Streep, just hoping for a chance for a fulfilling career. I didn't know what I was in for when I chose it.

No matter how hard I tried, I was never able to break into the Screen Actors Guild. Without being a union member, my pay scale was lower, and I wasn't eligible for health-insurance benefits. Also, SAG actors looked down on their non-union counterparts. I never felt as if I belonged.

I kept trying, but it was a catch-22: Only SAG actors were sent on SAG auditions, even though various agents I'd had promised to "slip me in" when they could.

To outsiders, these union distinctions were meaningless. Even Denise, my closest friend, thought of me as "an actress"— which, to many people, automatically means glamour, fun, and living the high life. She pointed out that even if the previous night's date wasn't so thrilling, I was never at a loss for men who took me to dinner.

"The men have different names, but really, it's like I'm dating the same person over and over," I said. "I'm not feeling a connection. I'm not feeling connected anywhere. Except for you, I don't feel close to anyone, not even my other friends. I was born in this city, but it all feels so transient."

Maybe I had no real ties at all, anywhere. Maybe I never did. Even though I was very close with my mother and still relied on her almost daily opinions about my life, she and my stepfather were now living in Florida. The room I stayed in when I visited them there was a generic guest room, not "my" room. It was wallpapered in a mosaic of dizzying, dispiriting brownish colors. It was not even my own room while I was there, because it was also home to my stepfather's computer, which he used every day. He and my mother did their best to make me feel like a welcomed guest, but that's all I was—a guest. That's how I felt everywhere I went, even sometimes in my own home.

I'm sure that this feeling stemmed in large part from when my parents separated and split the siblings up when I was six years old. It wasn't as if life was idyllic even before then, like when my father would demand a "fifteen-minute silent period" at every meal while my brother and sister and I tried not to further inflame whatever was going on between our parents. "Your father is tired and stressed," my mother would explain.

It wasn't so much the divorce that unseated me as for how my father took my two older siblings to live with him, leaving me with my mother. I felt as if he had divorced me, and separated me from my brother and sister, who were 15 and 12 at the time.

I don't remember how or even if this was ever really explained to me. My mother and I—along with our black mini poodle, Remmington—stayed at a nearby hotel for a few days, and when we returned, my father, brother, and sister were gone, along with all their belongings. The apartment felt vacant, although the furniture was still there. Even David's football and special coin collection were gone. It was as if they had never existed. I was scared and confused. I felt as if I'd been stripped clean of my entire family. Was it my fault? Had I done something wrong?

"Dad needs us, little one," David later told me. "He said he would die without us." Which left unanswered the question of how my father was fine living without *me*, and why neither parent balked at cutting me off especially from my brother David, with whom I was particularly close.

From then on, David and Deane were a pair. They had each other. They grew up together. They came over on weekends for "visits." They arrived together and left together, sometimes leaving early when my father called and said he "needed" them, including one time on my birthday. I felt like an only child.

I wasn't sorry to be with my mother. I loved her. I revered her. When she dressed for an event, she looked like a movie star in her pearl necklace and her V-neck, sleeveless, pleated dresses that cinched at her tiny waist. She always smelled of Joy perfume. She was regal in manner and taught me at an early age to send out thank-you notes the same day as receiving any gift. But the entire dynamics of the family changed overnight, and I found myself utterly dependent on her and her good will, with no one else to turn to when her ever-shifting mood changed.

I spent my childhood—and perhaps much of my adulthood—trying desperately to please or at least placate my mother. When I did manage to please her, I felt momentarily wanted and important. I felt safe.

"Your cousin Kiki is so smart. Brilliant, really," she said on more than one occasion.

"Yes, Mom," I said, dutifully agreeing with her even though each compliment she doled out to anyone else in the world took just a little more oxygen away from me.

Along with my growing dependence came frustration and anger whenever I felt her focus on me had drifted. "ALISON," she chastised me for my outbursts, drawing out every syllable, "*you are being very rude.*"

Within an hour I'd be tearful and contrite, trying to undo the harm I'd wrought, trying endlessly to atone. I couldn't apologize enough. One time I went down the block and bought her a bouquet of daisies with baby's breath, her favorite, using my allowance money. Then I searched the pantry for a box of Aunt Jemima and baked her a coffee cake. I served it to her in bed, the vase of daisies alongside it on the tray. I had to ensure that we were still connected, that she hadn't given up on me. I clung to her like adhesive, followed her around like a puppy. She was all I had.

It was my mother, it turned out, who had asked for the divorce. My father refused to grant it. When I was nine, my mother pulled me out of the exclusive Dalton private school on the Upper East Side and moved the two of us for nine months to an apartment in Las Vegas so she could formally end the marriage. Now I was separated from my sister and brother and also in a new city and a new school, mid-year. I didn't know a soul.

George, a man my mother had been dating in New York, flew out to Vegas to visit us a few times. He brought me the new Polaroid camera that had just come out, and I secretly wanted to love it, but I pretended it was just an okay gift because I was so jealous of the time he spent with my mother. She lit up when she saw him. He had a Woody Allen type of humor that made her laugh and laugh. I could hear her lovey-dovey voice when she was on the phone with him. I didn't want to share her with anyone.

My fears were well founded, in a sense. The minute the divorce came through, my mother announced that she would be marrying George. She called my new stepfather the love of her life, which I, of course, took as a way of disparaging me. I had failed to make it as the love of her life, while George made her happy. He was easily able to coax her from her bad moods, even on Sundays when they were at their worst. She was proud of my good grades, but to me, it didn't compare to how George could make her light up in a smile. I felt I had to make an appointment to be alone with her.

After my recurring nightmare, after my morning call with Denise, I continued to go about my ordinary chores, doing everything the same way I had always done it. I finished in time for my customary lunch at The Broadway Diner.

"What's it going to be, the usual?" the waitress asked me. "Chicken salad, whole wheat…"

"This time, no pickle," I said. Maybe that was the beginning.

2

I went to bed with my first love on our first date.

"What's wrong?" Jim asked me. "Why are you crying?"

"Maybe we went too fast?" I said, or asked, hoping for reassurance while worrying that I had already ruined everything. I was 23, but a *young* 23. Also, a proper enough young lady who sent out same-day thank-you notes, who didn't want a man thinking she was something she wasn't.

I called my mother, desperate for her advice, and hoping that she, too, would not think I was loose and immoral. "Don't call him," she said. "Let him come to you." That had always been her advice, whether I had just met a cute guy in the library at school or someone from a party. "Let him come to you."

I knew that my mother was right. I knew that succeeding at the dating game meant not jumping into bed with anyone too fast, but I was fully in love with Jim by our second date, when he held and comforted me for hours after my grandfather died. We were married two years later.

In another two years, we separated.

Sigmund Freud once said, "I cannot think of any need in childhood as strong as the need for a father's protection." If that was the case and a girl's first love is her father, I was in trouble.

I don't remember having a rewarding relationship with my father, David, before my parents separated. It deteriorated further from there.

My father looked good on the outside, with an athletic build, close-cropped hair, and an engaging smile. He was in advertising and was very good at selling, but when it came to me, he wasn't very good at delivering. Once he'd moved out with my brother and sister, he told me, "I'll be there," but then he wasn't. It was as if the rest of my family had been carved out and was living with a total stranger.

Even his gifts made me feel like an afterthought. "This is what he gave you for your birthday?" my mother asked as she examined a necklace he'd given me as a teenager. "They're just cultured pearls, and not very good ones."

Right after the divorce, my father tried to get all three kids into a "family photo," but the photographer couldn't get me to smile. I didn't feel like smiling. I always felt like crying. It was only my brother, David, who saw the real sadness in my eyes. "Hey, little one," he whispered. "You can do it. Give us a smile." For a brief moment, I was able to turn my lips upward just long enough to be memorialized in a photo that masked how deeply our family was fractured.

When I thought about my father or missed him, it was more like the idea of him that I missed. I longed for a fantasy, for an idea of a love that was enduring and unconditional. I daydreamed my way into happy, romantic movies, as if any photo of me smiling were on their mantels, not the one in my father's new apartment.

It was a girlfriend from college who introduced me to Jim, someone she had met while in law school. His voice on the phone was soothing. "I want to hear all about you," he said, music to my ears.

He was charming, intelligent, and we talked about our lives. He was flirtatious yet warm. I could almost hear him smiling at the thought of us meeting in a few months, once he had finished studying for the bar exam. I was smitten from that first phone call.

When we finally met in person, he did not disappoint. I felt an immediate comfort with him, not to mention the hypnotic pull of his aquamarine eyes. Those eyes never left my face, no matter which one of us was speaking. No one else in the room mattered.

There was no way to tell how much of my attraction was to Jim, the passionate Italian-American with the big family I wanted to be a part of, and how much of it was to the feeling he gave me, that feeling I had dreamed of since childhood, of someone making me the center of their universe. It didn't matter, because the feeling was mutual, or so it seemed.

After a year together, Jim moved in with me in my tiny first New York City apartment. I lay on top of him on the bed when we watched TV together, my head against his neck, totally at one with this man. He made me feel connected and important.

Still, the cracks began to show. He devoted himself to me … but he also devoted himself to his family, and I found myself once again in an emotional tug-of-war, trying to compete with all the competing claims on his attention. On his birthday one time we had big romantic plans. While he was still upstate visiting his parents, I tried on everything in my closet until I found just the right form-fitted sweater that hugged me in all the right places. I did a last-minute spritz of eau de parfum. Then he called to say he couldn't get away.

"But it's your birthday," I said. "We have reservations at 8. You should have been on the road by now."

"I know, hon, but my mom is making her special eggplant parmesan."

"But we have reservations at Plaza *España*," I repeated, not comprehending.

On the one hand, I was dating a man who cared about his mother, and that was certainly a good thing. On the other hand, we didn't speak for weeks after that.

We got through it. We had been together two years, including one year of living together, when he handed me a card that read, "To my love, will you marry me?"

"Yes, yes!" I cried. I wrapped him in a hug and kissed him with passion.

"Whoa," he said. "You don't have to give me your answer this minute. Take a few weeks."

"I don't need a few weeks," I said. "I've known since the beginning that you're the one for me."

We broke the news to my mother and stepfather first. "Oh honey," my mom said. "We're so happy! Although we're not surprised, I knew this would work out."

Then we called Jim's parents, all four of us on different extensions. When we told his parents, there was silence. "Are you there?" Jim asked.

"Yes," his mother said. "We're just … we're shocked."

My heart had been racing with excitement, and now it felt like something else. Dread, maybe.

"It's just that we'll have to adjust to our lives changing," his father tried to explain.

I was on the phone extension in the living room. Jim was in the bedroom. I couldn't see him from where I was standing, and I felt utterly abandoned. Why wasn't he speaking up? Why wasn't he telling them how much he loved me, how much he wanted to marry me? I wanted him to set the record straight right up front. But he didn't, and I dropped the receiver and ran to the bathroom, choking on my tears.

When we went to visit his parents upstate the following weekend, things were no better. They greeted me politely but spent a lot of the weekend walking aimlessly around their modest house in Hyde Park, looking miserable and forlorn, or like zombies after the apocalypse. They acted as if they were in mourning, on their way to a funeral. The funeral of their son, who had so sorely disappointed them in his choice of a bride, probably because I wasn't Italian like they were.

I was young. I didn't know how to handle it. I looked to Jim for reassurance, for guidance, but he didn't say anything and left me floundering. He couldn't even smile unless he felt sure that his parents were happy about our news, and that's when I knew that we had at least one thing in common—an inviolate need to please others, especially our mothers.

"Can't you just be happy for us?" I asked him.

"I need *them* to be happy," he said.

I had enough presence of mind to call off the engagement, although I was sick about it. I couldn't sign up to live for life in a household where I would never be my husband's top priority.

I wasn't eating. I wasn't sleeping. I didn't know what else to do so I went to stay with my mother and George in Florida, hoping that Jim would see that his life without me was empty.

He kept insisting he wanted me back, but somehow never managed to set a wedding date. When he finally did, I came home.

Jim's family never warmed toward me, except for his grandmother, who wrapped me in love from the moment I met her until the day she died. For her 80th birthday, I knitted her a stylish white wool and cashmere sweater, full of twisty cables, and with five fancy buttons. When she opened the box, she cried tears of real joy, and she wore that sweater constantly.

With Jim's grandmother, I had that familial feeling I had longed for and cherished, with the rest of the family, not so much. During our two years of marriage, Jim and I had increasingly nasty fights about the stranglehold I felt his parents exerted on our lives.

"I can't stand the way they control us," I would say.

"They just want to see us more often," Jim said.

"But I don't want to be put on a visitation schedule." It reminded of how my brother and sister had been scheduled to visit me dutifully on weekends.

After two years married and another two separated, we were divorced. I felt shattered that it hadn't worked out, and ever farther from my goal of a feeling of stability and belonging. I had been so sure of him at the beginning. How would I know how to choose better next time?

Soon after the divorce was final, a homeless man saw me moping along down the sidewalk. "Miss, you looking so sad," he said. "There is pain inside. There's no smile with you."

I gave him a few dollars and tried to fake a smile, but it felt foreign on my mouth. Even strangers on the street could see there was something wrong with me. Even a homeless man on a blanket on the pavement felt sorry for me.

I had to do something. I had to shake myself out of this funk.

I deliberately began flirting with guys again, in a kind of fake-it-till-you-make-it move. Flirting had always come easily to me. As children, my sister had been known as the smart one, while I was the pretty one—which made both of us unhappy and feel lacking. I went through life often setting my sights low to avoid the pain of finding out that it was true, that I wasn't smart enough. I only finished two years of college, leaving to become a flight attendant, not even considering some scholarly field because I feared I'd never make it.

Nevertheless, I'd never had trouble meeting men. Cute guys were everywhere. All I had to do was give one of them a wide-eyed look and he'd be right over to chat, whether I was on the shuttle to Boston to visit a friend, or at the neighborhood gym where, with the help of a bit of blush and mascara, I'd ask for help with one of the machines. It was as simple as that.

But still I was lonely.

Finally, a few years after my divorce, I met a man who made me feel safe and wanted. Larry was an art director ten years my senior who felt like a father figure. He was balding and had a deep bass voice that made me laugh. After a few months of casual dating, we became more intimate.

By now I was in my mid-thirties, and my hormones were in crave mode for a baby. But we had different long-term views of our relationship.

I lowered the volume on the TV; it was a commercial during "Shark Week" on the Discovery Channel. "Larry, we've been together two years," I said. "It's time to look, to think about, you know, having a baby."

Larry breathed out a fog of the pot smoke he'd been holding in. "I don't know if that's what I want," he said. "I don't think I'm ready."

"Okay," I said, wanting to be reasonable. A reasonable, understanding girlfriend. "When do you think you'll be ready?"

"Can't really say."

He lumbered to the kitchen and came back with another Eskimo Pie from the freezer.

I tried again. "Do you think you'd be willing to talk to someone about this?" I asked.

He reluctantly agreed to see a therapist to help him sort out his feelings on the topic. "Give me a year," he said.

I circled the date in red a year from then on my calendar and practically counted down the days. When that day rolled around, I broached the topic again.

"So what do you think, Larry? Is it time for a baby?" I asked.

"Huh?" he said.

"It's been a year. You said to give you a year!"

"Well, I've decided it's not right for me."

"What? But I gave you a year ... does this mean you're breaking up with me?"

"No, baby, not at all!" he protested. "Of course I still want to see you. Let's just keep it casual. It's fine the way it is."

Fortunately, my mother refrained from saying anything about why buy the cow when you can get the milk for free, but she didn't have to. I already knew that I came off as too needy—because I *was* too needy.

I had to change that. I needed to become someone I was not: independent. I had to get my brain to refresh so I could alter myself into that other kind of woman, the one who was too independent to worry about what a man thought of her.

That's what I would do. I would become the kind of independent woman that men wanted. I would start by going hiking in the Dolomites.

3

On the platform for the train to Bolzano, where I would be meeting the hiking group, I sighed loudly enough that a kindly gentleman inquired as to whether I was okay.

"*Signore.* Do you speak English?" I asked.

"*Si,* a little," he answered. I was grateful for that. I'd taken two semesters of Italian, but all that taught me was how to conjugate *andare,* to go, but not enough to engage in real conversation.

"The train was supposed to be here eight minutes ago," I said, looking worriedly at my watch.

He laughed. "*Signorina,* this is Italy. A eleven o'clock train do not mean eleven o'clock."

The Italians live a more relaxed existence. Few of them wear a watch, and everything is *dopo,* later. This is so ingrained in the Italian attitude that I doubt Mussolini would make the trains run on time if he were trying today. I would have to adjust my rigid self, or this trip would be even more stressful than it already was—traveling alone, with my historically poor sense of direction and little grasp of the language.

I was fixated on trying to find a new me, someone who could take a vacation like this on my own, with a group of strangers, and relax enough to enjoy myself. I had never done anything like this before. I always felt I needed to be attached to someone in order to travel anywhere.

By taking a hiking trip, I imagined I would become a more contemplative person. In the great outdoors, amid the beauty of the northeast Italian mountain range of the Dolomites, I would soul-search for a way to connect my body with nature. It would be therapeutic. Maybe I'd make some new friends. I would prove to myself that I could become my own center and not rely on my attachment to others to feed my sense of self-worth. This, at least, was the goal.

The train arrived in its own good time. Here I go, I thought. Off on a great adventure! I tried to pretend that my heart was light and carefree.

What was *not* light was my luggage. I could barely lift the humongous black American Tourister suitcase from where it was planted on the platform beside me. I had only packed the barest necessities: clothing, hiking gear, rain poncho. Plus my knitting, and a few books in those days before Kindle. My collection of what-if's: Ativan, anti-nausea pills, anti-diarrhea meds. Aspirin. First-aid items, nothing fancy—just bandages and gauze and tape. Antibiotic ointment in case I got blisters. Several pairs of shoes, because you can't just wear hiking boots to dinner in an Italian hotel.

Plus, my shoulder bag, which seemed to weigh just as much. In this, I wasn't alone. What was in it? I couldn't say. I see women listing to one side all the time from the weight of their shoulder bags. I'm surprised at the number of women who do *not* get rotator cuff injuries.

As I struggled to get the suitcase over the lip of the train doorway, a hand suddenly appeared. The conductor got me safely on board, but then I still had to yank and pull my luggage along a tight corridor to my designated seat, in a summertime train car without air-conditioning. *Per favore, aiutami. Qualcuno può aiutarmi??* Please help me. Is there someone to help me? This was how I began my journey toward becoming my own center—by begging strangers for help.

Two hours later, my worries faded away as the shimmering Italian Dolomites came into view. The sky in Bolzano was a brilliant crystal blue, the air crisp and clean. The town, in the Sudtirol region, is a blend of Italian and German, even in their signage, and I looked forward to hiking, and maybe even seeing the other sights there—some Giotto frescoes and a prehistoric alpine man whose body had been preserved inside a glacier.

First, though, overheated from the non-air-conditioned train ride, I changed into my new red bikini. I could always count on swimming to calm my nerves, and I couldn't wait to jump into the hotel's spotless, azure pool.

I knew I had a relatively good body—at least that's what everyone back home always told me— but I was put to shame by the chic Italian women poolside in their skimpy, stylish swimwear. Each one of them came like a matched set with a handsome Italian dreamboat by her side. These women happily flaunted their bodies. They all moved with grace and confidence, as if every one of them had been raised by a ballet mistress.

I felt exposed as a charmless American, alone and without style. I threw a robe over the bikini I had thought so beautiful when I bought it, whose tags I had so recently and eagerly removed in my room. It now struck me as hopelessly dowdy, a hand-me-down from some long-ago season.

I was still determined to swim. I knew I would feel better about everything once I got in the water, so I removed the robe, sucked in my tummy with every ounce of strength from all those abdominal crunches I'd done, and tried not to draw attention to myself as I stepped into the water.

I shrieked.

The pool here was not heated like the one at the gym back home. It felt like it was below freezing, like a glacier should have formed where an inflatable pool float was drifting by.

In the end, I bought a pastel silk scarf from the lobby gift shop and had the saleslady show me how to knot it the Italian way so it looked complicated, yet elegant. I practiced in my room for an hour. It helped to some extent when I ate dinner *da sola*, alone, later that night in the hotel's terrace restaurant, and when I sat in one of the lobby's large fluffy chairs for one of the two cigarettes I allowed myself each day.

By the next morning, the entire hiking group of 18 had arrived. At 37, I was in the midrange of the others, who were between 28 and 70 years old.

We met our two tour guides, Jenny and Brent. They were both North American, but Jenny—a petite woman from Maine, with athletic legs and not an ounce of body fat—wore a light-blue T-shirt that said Italia in white letters.

"Hey, all of you, welcome to the group," she announced. "Are you ready to have a super swell time?"

We all murmured that we were indeed ready for such a thing, and she had us say it louder and with more vigor.

Brent was the more soft-spoken guide, a young-looking 25-year-old from Minnesota who played mostly to the women in the group. "Make sure you look pretty during the hike tomorrow," he said.

Who was he kidding? I had come there to feel free and alive, not to have to worry as I usually did whether I was good enough or attractive enough to find the right kind of partner. For these hikes, I was willing to let it all go—hair in a ponytail beneath a baseball cap, rugged shorts, and a simple T-shirt. Okay, and a little lip gloss, but that was it. I didn't normally wear much makeup, but I felt naked without at least some-thing. It was bad enough that these hikes would be starting promptly at 7:00 a.m. each day. I have never been a morning person, so being ready and bright-eyed at 7:00 a.m. was like asking me to be a rocket scientist on short notice.

I had brought two alarm clocks, just in case I overslept. On the first hike, as I stumbled outdoors at 7:00 a.m. like a vampire getting caught in a blinding flash of daylight, I decided to stick close to Jenny. She was fluent in Italian and at ease in Italy, which I admired enormously, and she liked to chatter away, which meant far less conversational work for me until I was properly acclimated to the day.

"How do you like living in Italy?" I asked, and that was all it took. Jenny was off and running. Even on the steepest inclines, she didn't seem to break a sweat or huff and puff like I was doing.

Jenny had met her Italian husband, Filippo, at a friend's wedding in Tuscany. "I went nuts for him right away," she said. "He was different, more sophisticated than the guys back home." She learned Italian from him, and by speaking it as often as she could.

"Changing cultures like that, so difficult," I managed to say, my breathing labored. "I could never do a thing like that."

"Oh, you'd be surprised," said Jenny, and on she went about her move to Italy, her adjustment, and the easy, natural path of love that was meant to be. I did not have any vocabulary in any language to describe something like that in my own life, mainly since it had never happened to me.

Finally, it was my turn to speak, and there was only one thing I had to say. "Is there somewhere I can pee?" I asked. "I drank a lot of coffee at breakfast."

It was to be a recurring theme on these hikes in the days to come—how much coffee I required to get myself out the door so early, and how long it would take before I halted everyone's progression by needing to stop along the side of the trail, my Kleenex already at the ready.

Even by the end of the first day, I could swear that my thighs felt firmer. Even if I never got over Larry and my inability to be part of a solid couple, at least I was getting a real workout.

Every day that week was similar—up early, coffee and breakfast (with an emphasis, as far as I was concerned, on the caffeine), pick up our lunch at the supermarket, take a small bus to the trailhead, and then hiking all day, up toward sweeping grassland pastures, like something out of *The Sound of Music*. Sweet-looking cows, lowing at each other as they grazed. Nimble, silky-haired goats with their gently curved horns, frolicking. The scenery was spectacular, with white sprinkles of edelweiss and yellow cuppings of Alpine pasque. There were hanging violet clutches of delicate bearded bell-flower and sometimes even a rare silvery cranesbill.

There were rugged patches for us to traverse, too, and these I was not quite so fond of. I was aware of how much I slowed the group with my frequent caffeine pit stops. I tried to travel just as fast and surely as everyone else when I was *not* busy peeing, even when it came to the occasional rock scrambling, where we had to use our hands to help us up. I was eager to try. It made me feel like a real Alpinist. But I have to say that I was not good at rock scrambling, and no one who was on that trip would disagree. My hands got bloodied from the sharp rocks; my kneecaps, too. I don't know how the others managed. I ended each day filled with wonder and awe at the natural panorama, and mangled and bloody from the rock scrambling.

"Anyone going for a massage before dinner?" Jenny asked when we at last reached the peak, our designated lookout point, where we could gaze down on all that we had accomplished. It felt up there like we were closer to heaven, held aloft by the vertical mountain walls in their kaleidoscope of white, grey and pink. "How about you, Alison?" said Jenny. "You look a bit tired."

"I'm fine," I said. Really, though, all I wanted were the two evening treats I always promised myself: a glass of wine and a cigarette. I had gone far out of my comfort zone. Even to the point of indulging in the area's culinary delights that I never would never have allowed myself back home. The flakiest, most buttery *cornetti*, croissants; full-fat steamed milk in my morning cappuccino; perfectly al dente pasta with rich pancetta and a touch of extra-virgin olive oil; the freshest, milkiest mozzarella *di bufala*—but I could not leave every habit behind. I still needed to end the day with one glass of wine and one of my two daily allotted cigarettes. The entire week was fantastic, but it did not turn me into the different person I had hoped to become.

4

Before meeting the hiking group in Bolzano, I spent a day and a night in Verona, the city where Romeo met (and lost) Juliet. I made it a point to stand beneath Juliet's balcony, just like all the tourists do, even if the 13th-century Casa di Giulietta, on Via Cappello, cannot totally be verified as the house Shakespeare had in mind when he wrote his tragic love story, and even though the rectangular stone balcony was actually added on to the building in modern times. Gazing up at the balcony fires the imagination and stirs the heart even if there's no certificate of authenticity to its name.

I, too, felt the romantic pull: of history, of literature, and of the idea of a love worth dying for. What I hadn't counted on was how lonely and isolated this tourist attraction ultimately made me feel. In the courtyard below the balcony, couples kissed and kissed, while I stood around awkwardly, consulting my guidebook and my map. I had come to Italy in part to become more realistic about my romantic expectations, and here I was mooning over Juliet's balcony and the romantic ideal of a Romeo who would rather not live than live in a world without me.

Instead of a genuine Romeo, what did I have? I had two annoying young Italian *ragazzi*, street kids, who followed me as I walked to a solitary dinner at a local restaurant. They tracked my footsteps, tenacious and irritating like eczema.

Vuoi venire con me a cena? I recognized the word "*cena*," dinner. No, I would not like to have dinner with them.

I surreptitiously slipped off the gold band I had worn on
my right fourth finger since my divorce and moved it back onto
my wedding-ring finger. I would insist, in my limited Italian,
if I had to, that I was *fidanzata*, engaged. Simply putting a
ring on that finger calmed me down, gave me back the old
feeling of security, of being wanted, of being "taken." It was
the only language men like these *ragazzi* understood, so why
was it wrong if I believed in it too? Why was it wrong to pine
for that old feeling again, the certainty that a man loved me?

When I returned to my hotel, I happened to enter the
lobby at the same time as a tall, dark, slender Italian man. He
was immaculately dressed in a well-made navy blue suit and
classic brown leather tie shoes. He had a full head of thick
dark hair and his eyes, when he caught mine, were a sparkling
brown. After the ragazzi, this man looked classy and refined.
Plus, I already had my one nightly glass of wine in me.

I smiled back. I moved my ring to the other hand.

I spent the evening speaking in my bad Italian to Leonardo,
sometimes with the help of the Filipino bartender, who trans-
lated between us as necessary.

We both ordered Diet Cokes. I tried to explain how they
didn't have any sugar in them, and Leonardo kept trying to
have me pronounce the word for sugar correctly.

"*Zucchero*," he said.

"*Zuccarroh*."

"No, *zucchero*," he said patiently. My lips puckered as I
tried to say it again, and Leonardo leaned over and kissed me.

Amazing how my limited Italian suddenly improved. "*Hai
le labbra piu belle che abbia mai visto*," he said, placing his
finger on my mouth, and I knew exactly what he was saying.
I had the most beautiful lips he had ever seen.

He was gorgeous. He was Italian. He was suave and man-
nerly and appeared to be as interested in me as I was in him.

I felt like I had entered into the land of the romantic movies I had watched as a child. It was a place that allowed me to fantasize about what could be, and it was a place where I wanted to stay.

Even so, I had gnawing doubts. I was disappointed in myself. I had come here to go hiking and learn to stand on my own, and I had not been in Italy 24 hours, and I was already falling for some handsome stranger who I didn't know well enough that he could yet disappoint me.

On the other hand, this was Italy, the land of romance. I was acting instinctively. Wasn't that good? Wasn't I there to get out of my rut and learn to live life in the moment?

Whenever I entered this zone of intense romance, it gave me a short-term feeling of connection, like a drug. I felt wanted and at peace. It was better than a painkiller because it didn't make me numb. It made me feel alive. But when Leonardo indicated in his limited English that he would very much like to continue kissing me inside my hotel room, I knew better. I told him I could see him again when I returned after a week from my hiking trip.

He escorted me upstairs to my room and reluctantly bid me farewell. "I be here, outside your door, waiting for you," he said. I laughed, but I was still wide awake at 3:00 a.m., wondering if he meant it. I put on my robe and opened the door a crack and, *grazie Dio*, no Leonardo standing in the hallway.

Now my hiking trip was over, and it was time to meet Leonardo in Venice, as he had promised. "Do you think he'll show?" I asked the other hikers at our final dinner, at a charming restaurant in nearby Cortina, one-time host of the Winter Olympics. We had all given each other little gag gifts; mine was a map of the Italian Dolomites, a dig at my lack of direction. ("You should move here, you have a glow here," one woman told me. "I could never," I said. "I'm terrible with languages.")

"He'll never come," said one woman in the group, Betsy.

"I'm pretty sure he meant it," I said. "Do you think he'll get his own room?"

Betsy snorted. "He's Italian!" she said.

It was true that I'd had trouble getting Leonardo on the phone from the Dolomites. Maybe it was the connection, but he kept hanging up on me. I must have tried five times before I was able to make a viable connection with him.

"Hello, hello, Leonardo. It's Alison. Hello!"

"Alison!" he said. He sounded overjoyed to hear from me, and I put Betsy out of my mind.

He confirmed that he would meet me in Venice, just as he'd promised. He said he had reserved his own room; I later called the front desk at the hotel and confirmed it. Maybe I didn't know a lot about Italian men, but neither did Betsy.

It was 7:00 p.m. when the phone rang in my Venice hotel room. I prayed it wasn't Leonardo canceling.

It was Leonardo, and he was *not* canceling. He was confirming. "I come there *alle otto*, before eight," he said. His English and my Italian were just enough to piece it together, to make a plan.

I felt desirable. On fire. My handsome Italian stranger was taking me to dinner in the most romantic city in the world. He was coming for *me*.

I put on the one sexy dress I had brought on this trip—a black, low-cut, form-fitted number. I put on my black sling-back sandals and checked myself in the mirror several times. I puffed the second of my two allotted cigarettes and nervously gulped down a glass of white wine from room service.

Leonardo rang promptly at 8:00 p.m.

"I am here," he said. "*In quale camera vuoi incontrarmi?*" *Camera*, room. He wanted to know whether to meet me in his room or mine. Mine still smelled of my cigarette, so I told him we'd meet in his.

I brushed my teeth again. I popped a breath mint. I walked down one flight of stairs to his room, and he wasn't there. I knocked softly at first, then more forcefully, but no one answered.

Was he really here at the hotel, or was this an elaborate joke? I ran back to my room and called the concierge, who assured me that my friend had checked in. "*Certamente, signorina*," he said.

I brushed my teeth again. More pacing. At last, it turned out that we had misunderstood each other—that he had knocked on my door just while I had been knocking on his.

It was worth the wait. After I dashed back down to his room and he finally opened the door, he took me in, and his first words were "*sei cosi bella.*" He made me feel like a movie star. He said I was beautiful. It was a far cry from the boyfriend who readily pointed out a pimple on my chin—as if any woman ever needs reminding—or the ones who would say, "Let's go," without even looking at me after the time I had taken to dress up and look glamorous. I had boyfriends who stole more looks at themselves in passing glass windows than even looked at or complimented me.

The romance didn't stop there. On the hotel terrace, over champagne in fluted crystal goblets and against a fiery Venetian sunset, Leonardo did not take his eyes from me. Not once. He did not check his watch. He did not check out other women walking by. At dinner a short walk away, near the Piazza San Marco, I could barely touch my food. I could barely speak, and not just because of my bad Italian—his penetrating gaze left me speechless in any language.

Was I in a dream? Leonardo was effortlessly hitting every romantic cue I had ever hoped for. I didn't care if this kind of romance was considered "old-fashioned," in the negative sense, back home. I knew what made me melt, and this was it.

We walked in the nighttime square hand in hand. We listened to musicians in dinner jackets playing love songs on violins. I held onto Leonardo's shoulders as we danced against the backdrop of an incandescent moon.

We kissed, and I sunk my body into his.

Back at the hotel, suddenly nervous, I invited Leonardo to come to my room—but not for sex. I felt I had to draw the line at simply having an affair with a complete stranger. All I knew about him was that he worked in construction and lived in Rome. It wasn't much to go on.

He said he wanted to brush his teeth and then he would come up. This guy is really clean, I thought. He was forever spraying the Italian equivalent of Binaca in his mouth. He was not a smoker, barely drank, and said he took several showers a day.

When he came to my room, I thought it was charming that he seemed nervous, too, and didn't try to grab me. We ended up kissing and cuddling most of the night on the small antique love seat by the window. I could see love in his smile and could feel love in his touch, even if it were only for the moment.

"Can you come back again tonight?" I asked him in the pre-dawn light. I held my breath for his response.

He said he would.

At seven o'clock that evening my hopes had vanished. Leonardo had not come. He had not called. Despondent, I went out on the hotel terrace to nurse a glass of wine, alone.

But not alone enough, for there was Betsy, one of several people from the hiking group who were also staying in the hotel before leaving Italy.

"Did that man ever come to see you?" she asked.

I couldn't help boasting about it, to show her that she'd been wrong about him. "I had the most wonderful night with him last night," I said. "He might even come back tonight."

"Now you're just being silly," said Betsy, smug in her Gucci blouse and Prada sandals. "I know the way Italian men think. You'll never hear from him again."

"You don't understand," I said. "We had a magical evening. It was the most romantic night of my life."

"Frankly," she said, "I think you're a fool."

I've never been the kind of person who laces into someone, who tries to shame someone in public, or even in private. I was brought up well. I handled it the way well-brought-up girls everywhere have handled things—by doubting myself and beating myself up internally.

Maybe this horrible woman was right—I was nothing more than a romantic fool. I was someone other people should feel sorry for.

I didn't even allow myself the enjoyment of finishing my evening glass of wine. Instead, I hurried back to my hotel room so that I could cry into my pillow about dashed dreams and a loveless future.

And there, in my room, I thought I saw a mirage. On the desk was a gigantic, beautifully arranged bouquet of flowers. Long-stemmed roses, brilliantly purple orchids, and sprays of baby's breath, all in a hand-blown Venetian vase.

My fingers trembled as I took the note from the envelope. I had to rush downstairs to the concierge for help translating it.

Dolce Alison. Ho fatto tutto per tornare ma non è stato possibile. È stato bello conoscerti e sono sicuro di revederti a Roma o a New York. Un bacione, Leonardo.

He had tried to make it, but it wasn't possible. He would see me again, either in New York or Rome.

He signed it with a kiss.

I couldn't wait to tell my mother. No matter what she said, no matter how she responded, I already knew what I was going to do. I'd had a glow in Italy; everyone had said so. I would study Italian, I would buy a ticket, and by next spring I would be living in Rome.

PART TWO

PART TWO

5

Despite my previous career as a flight attendant, with all of its travel perks, I had never flown business class until the day I moved to Rome.

It was April 30, 1995, nine months after the hiking trip. I had gotten a good deal on the ticket and felt like splurging to mark the occasion: anxious me, bad with languages and directions, changing my life.

The airplane chardonnay was not bad, and it was served in a real crystal wine glass. The flight attendant brought me complementary socks for my feet and a headset for my listening pleasure. It all felt so luxurious. But it did not reduce my anxiety.

What was I doing? Why was I doing it? "I know I can't stop you when you're this determined," was my mother's basic take on my whole Italy plan, and I wasn't sure how much of that was a compliment.

Recently, I'd been having something new: panic attacks in the subway. "It's understandable before a big trip," one doctor said to me, but "big trip" sounded too small and ordinary to describe what I was doing.

"Do you have a job lined up?" people had asked me, but acting is not the kind of profession (or I was not the kind of actor) where you call up Martin Scorsese and ask him to reserve you a spot in the cast of his next film being shot overseas. I had the name of one theatrical producer, the ex-husband of a friend of my aunt's, and I had six months of savings, a can-do attitude, and a prescription vial of BuSpar for the panic attacks.

We were at 38,000 feet. I felt my fingertips digging into the armrests. I struck up a conversation with the young woman in the seat next to me, mostly to keep myself from hyperventilating and creating a scene.

Nancy was an effervescent African American who was living in Rome for her job at IBM. I told her I'd be looking for acting work once I got there.

"That sounds cool," she said. She wrote down her name on the back of her card. When she handed it to me, she must have seen the fear and panic in my face. "Don't worry, you'll be fine," she said. "There's a big ex-pat community there."

She took her card back and added her home number. I put it carefully in my wallet like it was a precious piece of gold.

"Are you fluent?" she asked.

"In Italian?" I almost choked on my wine. "I've been taking Berlitz ever since I booked this trip, but all I've gotten from it is 50 verbs. I had a private teacher for a while, but I still can't make a complete sentence."

"I have a friend, Flavia. She's good. I take lessons from her too," said Nancy.

Once I was certain that the plane was flying over land—somehow I thought it would be easier to survive a crash over Europe than over the open sea—I put on my headphones, put on some music, and shut my eyes. I found a channel that played '70s soul, and I drifted off to the Spinners singing "Could It Be I'm Falling in Love," while wondering whether moving to Rome just because Leonardo lived there was really a good idea.

Orlando, from the car service, met me outside the customs area with a placard that read Signorina Alison. He managed to stuff my many bags into his not-large Mercedes, although it blocked his view through the mirror, which only added to my stress. (If I overpacked for a one-week hiking trip, imagine what I did for an open-ended stay in Rome.) I explained away my nervousness and pale complexion with "*Sono molto stanca perche' non ho dormito ieri sera*," that I was very tired because I hadn't slept.

"*Lei parla Italiano molto bene*," he said, the first time anyone had told me I spoke Italian well.

As we drove along, I felt miserable—tired, confused, jet-lagged, and hoping that Orlando wouldn't need to use his rear-view mirror.

"*Ecco il Colosseo a destra*," he said, pointing to the Coliseum on the right.

I had seen it many years ago while visiting Rome with my mother and stepfather, but now it seemed so much bigger and dreamlike. "*Che bellissimo*," I breathed. Maybe someday I would actually feel at home here.

Orlando dropped me at The Residenza di Ripetta, an elegant, converted convent made into a residential hotel where I had reserved a room until I was able to get my bearings and figure out where I'd want to rent an apartment. It was a well-traveled area near the center of the city, close to the Spanish Steps, and on a pretty street filled with little gift, wine, and butcher shops.

My room was a large studio with high ceilings that made it seem even bigger. There was a queen-size bed on one side of the room, and a small couch and table by the window on the other side. I was used to the New York version of closet space—which is to say, none. Here there was an entire wall of smooth wooden closets and drawers that even my enormous suitcases couldn't fill.

It was bright and cheery and open. Thankfully, my window overlooked the quiet greenery of the courtyard, and not the honking of the cars and motorini scooters on the busy Via di Ripetta, where the best one could do to park was at a 45-degree angle because there was no room anywhere.

The apartment came completely furnished, right down to silverware, pots, pans, and plates. It was also equipped with a moka pot, a staple of Italian kitchens—but I was already worried that I wouldn't have access to my urgently needed morning coffee because I couldn't figure out how the device worked. The moka, or *macchinetta* ("small machine"), somehow sends steam through ground coffee—but it was unclear to me where to put the water, where to put the coffee, and how to turn the thing on. Even if I managed to get it on, how would I know when the coffee was done?

I turned to what I definitely knew how to do, which was unpack. This included removing and stacking cans of Bumble Bee tuna. Yes, I knew that Italy was famous most of all for its delicious food, but it was also famous for its olive oil and its abundance of cheese and for the Americans who visited there and packed on the pounds. I needed to make sure I'd have access to tuna in water, not oil. Maybe it was too much that I also brought along a dozen bagels from home, but I hadn't even unpacked the first of my five suitcases, and I was already feeling homesick. I was glad to have something familiar, even a New York bagel.

From another suitcase, I took out one of several photo albums I had packed. I missed my mother, but it was the middle of the night back home, and I couldn't call her. I missed hearing my brother, David, call me "little one." David lived about two hours north of my mother in Florida. I gazed at my most recent photo of him: tall and handsome, with windswept dark-blond hair and kind blue eyes. I felt that I could see the pain in those eyes, too—he had suffered for most of his life with Crohn's disease, and he lived with severe and chronic stomach pain. He never complained or put himself first, but just the knowledge of his illness created in me an endless pit of worry.

After unpacking bag number three I was exhausted, and I still felt I needed to call my mother. It was like craving one of my two cigarettes of the day, a habit I couldn't give up.

I went downstairs to look outside the hotel front door. The day had been dark and rainy, and although it had cleared up a bit, the city looked as if a bomb had gone off. It was the Italian Labor Day, and everyone had disappeared. There was no one walking on the street. All the windows were shuttered. None of the stores were open.

Nevertheless, I decided to take a walk in search of the local *palestra*, the gym. That would give me the comfort that my water-packed tuna and even the thought of talking to my mother couldn't do. Gyms were my main source for stress reduction. They got my endorphins going and made me feel human. In New York, I rarely skipped a day at the gym. It was my church, my haven, my safe place.

The concierge at the Residenza di Ripetta told me that The Roman Sports Center was the best gym in Rome, and would not be hard to find. It was owned by an American. "Walk toward Piazza di Spagna, and you will see two tunnels," he said. "Walk inside the tunnels for ten minutes, and when you get out, you will be near the gym." As he spoke, he gestured with both arms as if conducting an orchestra.

"Tunnels?" I said.

"Signorina, it is so simple. You cannot miss it."

Tunnels did not sound simple for me. I suffered from minor claustrophobia in the best of times, and lately from panic attacks in the New York subways. I wasn't sure I could manage "tunnels" my first morning in Rome.

My need for a gym outweighed my fears. I set out toward Piazza di Spagna, but either my anxieties kicked in or my horrible sense of direction because I could not locate these "simple" tunnels anywhere.

Instead, I walked up all 135 steps of The Spanish Steps. At least I got in my aerobic exercise for the day.

When I returned to Piazza del Popolo, the closest public square to my hotel, I noticed something odd. It looked like a staircase built right into the rocks. Although I had just finished with The Spanish Steps, I decided to explore this, too, one crooked step at a time, all the way to the top, huffing, and puffing.

The steps were steep and curved. They were steeper than The Spanish Steps, and there were more of them.

It was well worth the climb. At the top, it was as if I had entered another world in 3-D. The hill itself—it was called Pincio, I later learned—seemed to spill out in all directions. In the distance, I could see the Vatican and St. Peter's Bascilica. Over there was the "wedding cake" monument to Victor Emmanuel. I could see an abundance of other piazzas; indeed, I could see the entire city.

The sun had now fully come out, and everything was sparkling. I was beaming.

I savored the moment.

6

The next day the people had returned and the stores had reopened. It was time to *fare la spesa*, go food shopping.

There was an *alimentari,* a tiny food shop, right next door to the Residence. It was jam-packed with shoppers after the holiday weekend, and there was nowhere to put my items except to hold them in my arms, but convenience was key.

The minute I walked out of the store with my purchases, the fragile bag ripped and everything I'd bought was on the sidewalk or on me—including splattered vinegar and olive oil. I walked right back into the store, but the owner unsmilingly shrugged his shoulders. They didn't offer to replace a single item, and I had to buy everything all over again. I felt I was the *straniera,* the stranger from America.

Frustrated and caffeine-deprived, I dropped off my second round of groceries and took a short walk to find a store that sold coffee beans from around the world. I bought one bag of Italian decaf espresso and another of American coffee and steeled myself for trying to figure out how to operate the moka.

The *fuso orario,* jet lag, was bad. At the same time, too much caffeine would only fuel my ever-present anxiety, so I planned to mix the two grinds. I used one of the tiny teaspoons that the Residence had given me and filled the minuscule compartment of the moka, but while I was putting away the food I had bought earlier, I let the coffee boil too long. All the water burned out of the pot and the coffee had evaporated, leaving behind a burnt smell. I tried not to read into it, but it was my first official day living in Rome, and I couldn't even make myself a decent cup of coffee.

What I needed was to find that gym. Today. With determination, I once again set out along the route the concierge had described.

This time I located the tunnel. It began at the Metro station at Piazza di Spagna, near the Spanish Steps. I had walked right by it without noticing the previous day. The entrance was down a vertiginous, super-long escalator that happened to be out of order that day. At the bottom, I was to walk at least half a mile underground until I got to the parking lot at Viale del Galoppatoio, inside Villa Borghese, and then climb back up to street level where the gym was.

I successfully navigated the long, stalled escalator down into the domed tunnel. I don't know how far into the tunnel I got because I immediately began to feel that hot, choking sensation of claustrophobia and panic. That I seemed to be the only person down there, in a tunnel that stretched ahead of me forever, did not help.

I tried all the breathing exercises I had practiced back home, but it didn't help. My hands felt numb, which meant I was probably hyperventilating. I had to kneel on the ground and take long deep breaths until I could reasonably trust myself to turn around and flee back the way I had come, back up into the brilliant Roman sunlight.

The doctor I had seen in New York had also suggested that these attacks weren't just about moving to Rome, but also the idea of being so far from my mother. It was my lifelong fear, ever since my parents separated when I was six, that there was no place or person to ground me. The doctor gave me homework to do every day to face my "fearsome places and situations," but I didn't see how all the breathing exercises and behavior modifications and even anti-anxiety meds in the world were going to help a full-grown adult who couldn't go a day without calling her mother. I wondered briefly whether my move to Rome had something to do with trying to sever that umbilical cord once and for all as for anything else. If so, as of Day 2 the plan wasn't working.

I ate dinner alone that night at a touristy-looking restaurant around the corner from my hotel. The menu was prominently displayed outside the door—half in English and the other half in Italian.

I ordered prawns, and when the waiter brought them, I was aghast—the shell and head were intact. The creature's small black eyes stared up at me from the plate. I had no idea how to peel them or eat them.

"Pardon me. Do you speak English?" I asked the couple seated next to me. "I'm so embarrassed, but ... could you please show me how to eat these things?"

"Give me your plate," the woman said.

I handed it to her, and she skillfully peeled away all that one was not supposed to eat. I felt the waiter watching me, probably thinking that I was just another dumb American tourist who didn't belong here. Maybe he was right.

After that, I became consumed with finding a way to get to that gym. I needed a familiar place to check in every day. I needed the exercise to keep my weight under control with all the pasta I would undoubtedly be eating.

Above all, it was a point of pride. I had come all this way to start a new life, and I was going to start it with a gym membership if it killed me.

I was terrible with maps. I was terrible with directions. Nevertheless, I studied a map and walked outside to the main street, Via del Corso. From there, I thought that maybe I could get to the gym by walking up through Villa Borghese.

I got as far as a wide intersection and couldn't cross. Horns blasted, and cars sped by from every direction. No one stopped for me. After a few petrified attempts to cross, even with the traffic light in my favor, I tried something else. I held my hand straight out in front of me and made eye contact with the drivers—and, presto, the cars miraculously stopped. Had I discovered a secret? Feeling very accomplished, I decided that was enough for the day and that I would get even further the next.

That night I slept fitfully. I awoke multiple times, sweating through my nightgown. I climbed out from under the sheets and lay on top of them, listening for the sound of the air conditioner. It was silent. Had it stopped working? *Mio dio*, I couldn't survive the summer without air-conditioning. In the morning I found out that the management shut it off during the night unless they felt it was needed. They didn't feel it was needed yet.

I was not going to let a poor night's rest ruin my day. I marched over to the neighborhood *tobacciao* that sold bus tickets, candy, mints, stamps, and of course tobacco. I thought that buying a monthly bus pass instead of single tickets each time I had to go anywhere would make things easier for me. I handed the man behind the counter a fifty-*lire* bill, about thirty U.S. dollars.

"*Checosavuole?*" He spoke quickly, not even looking up at me. My heart beat wildly. I couldn't understand a single word. I couldn't even manage to buy a bus ticket. I was so, so hopeless.

Even so, I persisted, reciting the phrase I had practiced several times before the mirror. "*Per favore, vorrei comprare un biglietto mensile per l'autobus.*" I spoke as rapidly as I could because there were ten people pushing to get past me at the counter.

He must have understood me because he gave me the correct change along with my monthly pass.

I smiled broadly even as someone shoved me out of the way. I felt as if I had completed an Ironman competition. Maybe

I wasn't the winner, maybe I didn't come in first—but look at me with my new Italian bus pass! Now I would be able to ride up into Villa Borghese and find the gym.

I couldn't wait to show off my new bus pass to Francesca, a friend of my former Italian teacher in New York. Francesca lived in Rome and spoke fluent English. She had agreed to meet me for lunch and offered to show me around the affluent shopping area called Via dei Condotti.

I took my first bus, from nearby Piazza del Popolo to the famous Via Veneto, proudly displaying my pass to the driver. He did not seem very interested in looking at it. I held it up higher, right in front of his face. "*Lo vede?*" Do you see it?

The driver smiled at my innocence. "*Venga*," he said, the formal way to say come in.

The people behind me were shoving to get on board. We were all supposed to move toward the middle and validate our tickets at the ticket machine, but it was too crowded. It was even tilting to one side with so many people. I feared it might tip over. From the minute I got on people were pushing to get off, shouting, "*Scendi? Scendi?*" Are you leaving?

There was no air-conditioning here, either, and the open windows allowed in puffs of hot smog. Overall, this was not much better than the tunnels.

I told Francesca about it over a plate of linguine at the touristy Harry's Bar on the Via Veneto.

"Oh, the bus," she said. "They never ask for your ticket. No one monitors."

"Why would anyone buy a ticket, then, if they never check it?"

"I'm not sure anyone does. Perhaps that is why our transport system is almost bankrupt."

Francesca was a meek girl with smart clothes and bad skin. She loved to shop, and it was fun and comfortable to be with her and imagine myself having a circle of Italian friends. I would go broke, though, if I kept eating this way because our linguine turned out to be rather expensive.

I told her how I'd been obsessing with finding the Roman Sports Center.

"*La Palestra?* Roman Sports Center?" she said. "I know that place."

"It's complicated getting there."

"No, it's not."

"Really," I said. "I've tried."

"I will take you," she said. "I will show you."

She walked briskly through the streets, explaining each turn as we made them. "*Eccoci. La palestra,*" she said, pointing to the gym.

It had been a hot walk, and I was feeling weak. I looked forward to the blast of cold air-conditioning that was a staple of every health club in the U.S.

Not so at the Roman Sports Center, the best gym in the city. The air inside was stale and stuffy.

"*Non ha aria condizionata?*" I asked the person at the reception desk, but they, like the Residence, didn't turn on the AC until later in the season.

I joined anyway. The price for four months was a million *lire*, the equivalent of $650. There was also a mandatory stress test for an extra $100, which consisted of riding a stationary bike for 20 minutes. Now I was an official member of the Roman Sports Club. I belonged somewhere in Rome, if only for five mornings a week. I even found another route back to Piazza del Popolo by going through Villa Borghese. It was a beautiful walk, right out of an Impressionist painting, with children riding tricycles and couples strolling peacefully. It only took 25 minutes. When I again came to the busy thoroughfare, Piazzale Flaminio, I tried my new trick of holding out one hand while locking eyes with the drivers, and they stopped for me, so I could cross the street.

The next morning, I measured out two teaspoons of Italian decaf espresso and one of American coffee. As soon as the tiny aluminum machine had steam coming out of its spout, I turned off the heat. While it only made enough for one normal-sized cup of coffee at a time, I had mastered the art of the moka. It represented sure progress in my Italian education.

7

After the first few days of adjustment, I decided to branch out a little. I began walking along the Tiber River in the mornings to clear my head and supplement my visits to The Roman Sports Center, as a way of getting exercise and being in a familiar place. I had started taking Italian lessons from Flavia, the woman that Nancy on the plane had recommended. Italian is the most beautiful language in the world, and I wanted to know it well enough that I could begin to make my way in my new country.

Flavia agreed with my plan to venture further from Piazza del Popolo. On a day with a brilliant robin's-egg-blue sky, I set out to visit the Vatican. It was an easy forty-five-minute walk that curled left and followed the banks of the river. I crossed over at the Ponte Sant'Angelo, the most famous bridge in Rome, adorned by ten angel sculptures designed by Bernini.

The Vatican is a walled city of 110 acres. Not all of it is open to the public, but visiting it certainly takes more than a day. I singled out the Basilica of St. Peter so I could see Michelangelo's Pietà.

I was not the only visitor with this in mind. The crowds pressed on all sides of me as I tried to tamp down my claustrophobia and focus on how I was in the presence of one of the greatest sculptures of all time. I tried to ground myself in physical observations, like how my feet were planted firmly on the ground, and how the Carrera marble sculpture was securely encased inside a glass compartment and how surprisingly small it seemed up close. From photographs, I'd always imagined the Pietà as something immense that would take up an entire building, but in person, at just about six feet tall at its highest, it seemed almost tiny. In any case, I could not fully appreciate Michelangelo's artistry under these tense circumstances, the crowd swarming and pushing like an undulating being of its own, a boa constrictor of humanity about to cut off my oxygen. I supposed there would always be a crowd no matter when I came or what time of day, but it gave me at least a modest pleasure to know that I had something the tourists didn't—many opportunities to try again.

This was my home now. I belonged, and they were the visitors.

I had been in Italy a week now, and it was high time I saw Leonardo. He was only part of the reason I had moved here, but he had very much to do with why I chose Rome, a city with much to recommend it, but chiefly that it was the city that Leonardo called home. I had asked my Italian teacher in New York to contact him when she was in Rome on vacation and arrange the date for me because I'd had trouble reaching him and didn't have enough Italian to handle such a complex transaction. "He will meet you at the Residenza di Ripetta a few days after you arrive," she reported back.

I was thrilled at the thought of seeing him again. In his way, he had made all of this possible for me by showing me how it might feel if I were living the life of my dreams. My teacher taught me to say, *"Non vedo l'ora di rivederti. Ci vediamo oggi all'una a pranzo."* I am looking forward to seeing you again. I will see you at 1:00 p.m. this afternoon for lunch. I practiced those two lines for weeks before arriving in Rome, and it was the message I left on Leonardo's cell phone the morning we were to meet.

Would he show up? Maybe yes. Maybe no. I recalled Betsy, the woman from the hiking trip, and tried to prepare myself for possible disappointment. If he did show up, at least I would have a chance to assess his situation in more detail. Did he live with his mother, as many grown, unmarried Italian men did? Or was he married? If not married, did he have a special *ragazza*, a girlfriend?

I had been waiting near the *ingresso*, entrance, of the Residence on one of their overstuffed chintz sofas since 12:45. Now it was 1:20, which was not yet "late" by Italian standards, but I was getting nervous. At least the air-conditioning worked in the lobby.

Every now and then I ran to the ladies' room to check my hair. Finally, I went to the concierge desk and asked if there had been a call for me.

"No, *signorina*," he said. "*Nessuno*." No one.

Back to the sofa. Checked my bag again for lipstick and Altoids. Back to the concierge. "Nothing yet," he said in Italian before I even asked.

I could feel the first tear starting down my cheek when the manager, Mrs. Hirsch, happened to pass through the lobby.

"What is wrong, my dear?" she asked me, seeing my look of distress.

Although embarrassed, I let it all spill out. Mrs. Hirsch, bless her heart, got a hard look on her face. "This boy, he is Italian?" she asked. "Give me his number, *per favore*."

I followed her to her tiny office behind the concierge area where she dialed Leonardo's number and let him have it. Since she let him have it in Italian, I didn't know exactly what she was saying, but after she hung up, she turned to me and said, "Your Leonardo will be here in twenty minutes."

Thirty minutes later, he arrived, the same tall, dark and handsome man I remembered. The same penetrating eyes. If Mrs. Hirsch had unsettled him, he didn't let it show. After we kissed hello—one kiss on each cheek—he put a hand over those penetrating eyes. "I so sorry I am late, but my car is broken," he said.

I didn't believe him, but I was still glad to see him.

He took me down the street to Rosati for lunch. For the first time since coming to Rome, I wasn't hungry, but we ate two tiny panini sandwiches while standing alongside the bar, just like true Italians.

It was too noisy to talk, so we smiled at each other a lot. After we ate, he kissed me and asked if he could come see me the day after next.

"*A che ora?*" I asked. What time?

"*Presto. Alle dieci.*" Early, at 10:00 a.m.

"I have a question," I said. "Do you have a girlfriend?"

"*Beh*, I have a girlfriend, but we are not serious."

Of course, he had a girlfriend. Why wouldn't he? A handsome guy like that, he probably had several. He could even be married, for all I knew. Unless Mrs. Hirsch came along on our dates and stood at the bar eating paninis with us, I would probably never know very much about Leonardo.

As he left on his motorbike, he said he would call me *domani*, tomorrow.

He didn't.

Fortunately, it does not take long in Rome before meeting someone new. I was peacefully eating my salad and pasta at a nearby *trattoria*, beneath a pergola of flowers, when an attractive blond Italian man with a solid physique came over to introduce himself. He must have heard me speaking in English to the waiter.

"You are American?" he asked. "I am Rocco. I don't want to bother you. Here is my card, and if you need anything you can call me. I can help you if you want."

"I've just moved here from New York and don't know anyone yet," I blurted out. It was a dumb thing to say to a stranger, but I was tired, and he seemed so sincere. His English was a whole lot better than my Italian.

I took Rocco's card, and by the next morning, while taking my now daily constitutional along the Tiber, I was already daydreaming about him. Would he turn out to be a good guy and help me get used to life in Rome? Would he become my next boyfriend? I knew I shouldn't be thinking like this, back in the old dreamy romantic way, but it was relaxing, like stepping into a warm, familiar bath. On the one hand, Rome represented a new life that I had hoped would change me into that independent minded woman who didn't need a man to make her feel special but here I was, back on fantasy. Thanks to my absent, now deceased father for that.

I had told Rocco where I was staying, and the next day he called and asked me to lunch at Dal Bolognese, a chic place at the corner of the nearest square, Piazza del Popolo. The restaurant was filled with women in oversized tortoise-shell Audrey Hepburn sunglasses. They were dressed in sexy Dolce and Gabbana and carried Prada bags. I wasn't quite up to their level of chic, but I wore a celadon pantsuit my mother had bought me right before I left for Italy.

Rocco arrived right after I did, looking handsome in a blue sports jacket and classic beige slacks. For reasons I did not understand, he had brought along a sidekick, Angelo, who did not utter a single word throughout our lunch. I was confused about whether this was a date, or whether Rocco had meant what he said about being a friend, someone who was here for me whenever I needed.

"Angelo owns the best pizzeria in Rome," Rocco said.

"Oh, that's very nice," I said. What else could I say?

We dined outdoors beneath a white canopy, just me, Rocco, ... and Angelo. I didn't know what to think.

"Let's all get the grilled *pesce spada* and some fettuccine with just a little olive oil and garlic," Rocco said.

"Great, I love swordfish," I said.

"How about some white wine?" he added. I never drank at lunch, but I accepted a glass anyway. I wanted to feel Italian.

We toasted to new friends—to me, to Rocco … and to Angelo, whoever he was.

Rocco was the perfect gentleman. At the end of the meal, he grabbed the check. He invited me to dinner at his club that evening at 10:30 p.m.—Italians tend to eat very late—and said he would pick me up in his red Corvette, but eating so late at night was the one thing I was disliking about Rome. All I wanted to do at that hour was zone out on my bed to Italian TV (none of which I understood) and eat exactly six of the thick, moist Italian biscotti I was newly hooked on. I politely turned down his invitation and was content that night with my takeout rotisserie chicken and my six biscotti and with watching Italian TV infomercials for buttock trimming. I hoped Rocco would call again, but I wasn't sure I wanted to share another meal with the silent and mysterious Angelo.

My resolve broke down soon after. Evenings were lonely. A few days later, I called Rocco, fishing for an invitation. "Do you know of a good movie to go see nearby?" I asked.

"I can come take you to one," he said, just as I'd hoped.

He picked me up at 9:00 p.m. in a black SUV that I liked better than the flashy red Corvette. He looked boyishly handsome and was clearly in a good mood, singing in the car, joking with the waiters he knew at the restaurant where we went to eat, an Italian version of The Broadway Diner back in my days of chicken salad on whole wheat toast with lettuce and tomato. We sat at the counter on stools that twirled.

After a dinner of moist, juicy chicken with a glazed crispy glazed skin, we walked across the street to a theater that was showing Dustin Hoffman in *Outbreak*, a movie based on the book *The Hot Zone*, about the Ebola virus. Perhaps not the most romantic choice, but better than another night watching Italian TV.

I watched in amazement as Dustin Hoffman opened his mouth and out came perfect Italian, and in a much deeper pitch than I remembered from *Marathon Man*. "All the movies here are dubbed," Rocco explained to me in a whisper. "We do not believe in subtitles."

Still, I was happy. I liked being with Rocco. I was on a real date, and he had been a gentleman. He opened car doors for me, paid for my dinner and movie, and was always on time.

I did think it was strange, though, that when the movie was over, and he dropped me back at the Residence, he didn't even try to kiss me on the lips. Everything was topsy turvy in this country.

8

On Mother's Day, I missed my mother. It was way too early to call her in Florida. David still called me every few days—"Hey little one, it's the big brother calling"—but on this Sunday, while I thought about all the other families celebrating back home with all the other mothers, I needed to hear a familiar voice right then, not five or six hours of time zones from then.

When my parents separated when I was six, splitting up the family and divvying up the children, my mother would tell me, "I will never give you up. You must always know that. You are my little girl." Even then, I would feel fear and panic rather than comfort at those words. Her reassurance, in its way, implied that there was a real danger that it might happen, that unseen forces were right then arraying themselves against us staying together, that she might give me up after all. I slept with a nightlight on for the next several years.

Mother's Day, decades later, and I still felt the same fear and panic. It happened at times like these when it seemed I had no access to her. It happened when I tried to make a major life decision (or even something lesser than that) without first checking in with her. I was a grown woman, already divorced, living on my own in a foreign country, and I still felt I could not make a move without my mother.

While sitting alone in my room at the Residence, I went through my address book over and over, trying to find anyone I could call. I didn't know whether it was because I craved company or because hearing a known/familiar voice would make me believe I was still here on this earth, an affirmation that I existed.

I tried looking through Italian fashion and gossip magazines to fill the void of my lonely Sunday morning: *Gente. Italian Vogue.* I tried some sightseeing, to feel a part of Roman culture. I walked to Castel Sant' Angelo, a cylindrical castle that had originally been a mausoleum for the Roman Emperor Hadrian and his family. It was particularly beautiful around sunset when the sky outlined the castle in swirls of pastel against a crisp orange glow.

I tried, but I was always *stanca*, tired. I was in awe of the Italians, who seemed forever on the move, whether by foot or astride their little scooters as they zigzagged in the traffic. The women cooked dinner every night with seeming ease— delicious feasts with multiple courses. Everyone there loved to talk, and the Italian lent itself to creating long, luxurious passages to explain what in English would take a short, curt sentence. All this liveliness all around me, while I needed a nap each afternoon just to get through a single day.

The only time I didn't feel tired and alone was when I was at the gym, and not only because of the endorphins from the workout. It was also the company I had there, the familiar faces. The feeling of belonging.

"Welcome," the personable American owner, Ned, would always say when I checked in. He reminded me of Jack LaLanne with his muscular yet slender build. His wife, an attractive redhead named Amelia was also an owner, although she had her favorites and tended to welcome the guests selectively.

Manuel, a friendly and robust Peruvian trainer on the floor, was always introducing me to the other members. "How are things going, lady?" he would say to me affectionately. "*Voglio presentarti Alison. Lei è un' Americana. Una straniera."* *Straniera*, stranger. That's essentially what I was to them, even if the gym came closest to making me feel like part of a community.

I now was in the habit of taking the bus back to Piazza del Popolo, thus avoiding tunnels and crowded intersections. I think I was the only person who followed the rules about entering the bus from the front and descending via the middle door. I might have been the only one who actually paid for my ride.

Still, the isolation built up. I had forgotten most of the Italian I had tried to learn in preparation for the move. I felt overwhelmed by how quickly the Italians spoke, to the point where I could barely make out individual words.

Fortunately, my new Italian teacher, Flavia, was vibrant and bubbly and always managed to reassure me with her smile. Her demeanor was soothing.

"*Per favore*, do you *vuoi sederti*, to sit, here?" I asked her at my lesson. I was speaking poorly, becoming flustered.

"*Ciao bella*," Hello, beautiful, she said. "Try to tell me all in Italian, no English today, *va bene*?" All right?

"Okay," I said. "I mean, *sì*."

"*Come stai oggi*?" How are you doing?

"*Beh, non sto molto bene. Mi sento trieste.*" I am not doing so well. I am feeling sad.

"*Per favore fammi un sorriso.*" Please give me a smile.

The waterworks started. I burst into tears.

"*Cara*, what is the matter?" she asked me, looking alarmed.

"*Non lo so che cosa accadrà ... qui.*" I don't know what will happen here.

"*Non possiamo mai sapere cosa accadrà, cara.*" We never know what will happen, dear.

I let it all out. "I'm so overwhelmed that I moved here," I sobbed. "I can't sleep because the room is stuffy and they won't turn on the air-conditioning. I don't understand the guys who ask me out. I meet people, but I'm not making any friends. They call me *straniera*, the stranger."

Flavia comforted me. "*Sei bravissima*. You're very good. And you are very *coraggiosa*, brave, to be here alone," she told me. "Also, your Italian is improving, bit by bit."

"It is?" I asked hopefully, between sniffles.

"*Sì*," she said. "And I will help you, my dear."

That did the trick. Just the thought that someone out there would help me, look after me, immediately calmed me down.

Flavia was an angel. A mother figure. Flavia was nurturing, and I soaked it up.

Knowing I had someone to look out for me, I felt more confident. I realized that even if I hadn't made what I'd considered close friends, I had unwittingly become part of several social groups, which were more common in Italy—packs of acquaintances who dined and hung out together.

I was not used to going out with groups of friends. It was not the way things were in New York. However, I did my best to try and fit in, usually going along with whatever plans the group made, which invariably involved eating dinner at a time of night I would have preferred to be in bed. When they only spoke in Italian, I was at a loss, but usually several of them would know enough English to keep me in the loop.

One of these evenings, Luigi drove me back to the Residence after a group dinner. Luigi, a sweet jokester whose English was not terrible, was someone I had been introduced to by someone else, whom I had met through yet another someone else. I felt that connecting to all these Italians was just as important as my trying to feel accepted in all my Americanness, but I still didn't really understand how everything worked; socially and otherwise.

"Luigi, I wonder why everyone wants my number and says they want to invite me to everything," I asked.

"*Tu sei il mito Americano*," he said. You represent the American Myth.

He paused for a moment. "*Sai, gli Italiani portano maschere. Non dimenticarlo.*" The Italians wear masks. Do not forget that.

"What do you mean?" I asked.

"Many of us are very false people," he said.

I didn't know why he would say that or what, exactly, he meant—although I did feel that he was trying to look out for me, in a sweet way. It made sense that I represented to Italians a mythical idea of what an American is, just as some of them probably represented my own conception of an Italian myth.

The problem, though, with being a mythological creature to someone is that you are not then seen as fully human, with feelings and needs, and deserving of respect. At my next lesson, I asked my teacher Flavia for help crafting what I would say to Leonardo the next time I spoke with him: *Non posso credere che tu ti sia comportato tanto male con me. Sono molto delusa e penso che tu sia uno stronzo.* I can't believe your bad behavior toward me. I am very disappointed and think that you are a jerk.

I was really making progress in my conversational skills. Now I would be able to yell at Leonardo in Italian, even if I had to use my notes.

That is, if he ever called again.

9

I was finally about to meet with Gianmarco, a well-known theatrical producer and my one possible business contact in Rome. I had spoken with his ex-wife in the States before moving here, and she promised he would try and help me if he could. Since then, I had fantasized that this first meeting would be filled with exciting news of career opportunities. It would mark the beginning of my new success story in a foreign land.

I took a long shower to calm my nerves and tried on three different outfits before I settled on black slacks and a red top. Would he like me? Would he help me find work? I couldn't stop the anxious drumbeat in my head.

He was only twenty minutes late for our 8:30 p.m. dinner meeting, which I had learned was not at all bad in Italy. He had chosen an outdoor restaurant called *Due Ladroni*, Two Thieves. We sat awkwardly facing each other as I smiled and forced myself through the small talk, my stomach aching from anxiety.

"The Italian political system is a failure," he said.

"Even without Berlusconi?" I asked, which right away depleted my entire store of knowledge on the topic.

"It's still awful, corrupt," he said.

"Well, at least the fish here is tasty," I said nonsensically. "How's yours?"

"About the work situation for actors in Italy," he said. I perked up and leaned toward him. "It's terrible."

My shoulders sagged, "Terrible?"

"There is no work for actors," he said. "You are right, the fish is good."

I had built up this meeting in my mind for so long that I struggled to take in what he was saying. "Do you mean I will never find work?" I asked.

"I will try and introduce you to agents here in Rome," he said.

"Oh, that's great! Thank you so much!"

"And also in Milan. You would probably have a better chance in Milan."

"Milan?"

He pushed his plate aside and lit a cigarette, breathing out multiple puffs of smoke on each exhale. "There is nothing going on here in Rome," he said before another series of puffs.

I was barely managing to acclimate to Rome. I didn't relish the idea of up and moving to Milan, which was otherwise a four-hour train ride away. "You know agents in Milan ... for me?" I asked timidly.

"Not sure. Maybe."

He invited me to join him and an actor he knew for drinks later that night, but I begged off. All I wanted was to return to my room and my six biscotti.

When I returned to my room, a fuse had blown. No TV, no radio, no phone. *Niente.* Nothing. With nothing else to do, I drifted into a fitful sleep.

Finding a job was one problem among many that I faced, some of them bureaucratic. Anyone who comes to live and work in Italy needs a document known as a tax card, a little like a U.S. Social Security card. The tax office issues these cards, which come with a 16-digit alphanumeric code. Without it, I wouldn't be able to open a bank account, sign a lease or arrange for gas and electric—let alone secure employment.

Even if Gianmarco had showered me with my choice of roles in top movies being filmed in Italy, I still couldn't work without this card.

It was Rocco who had made me finally understand how important it was to obtain this card, and who confirmed my suspicions that getting just about anything done in Italy was a bureaucratic nightmare. "I am going to help you with it," he told me after calling one day and waking me from my daily *pisolino*, nap.

"*Grazie*, but I don't have any work yet," I said. "I don't know if I'll ever get work."

"You must have this," he insisted. "I have a friend who can help. He works in Vatican City."

Rocco kept his word. He took me the following morning to an office building on one of the streets near St. Peter's Basilica, where we met with his friend who would expedite getting me the tax card. All I had to do was fill out some forms, none of which I understood. I was grateful that Rocco was there to show me what to fill in and where to sign, and had to trust that he was not having me sign some illegal or nefarious document.

An hour later, his friend returned and handed me a green-and-white plastic rectangle that looked like a credit card. It said it was from the Ministero delle Finanze and had an official *codice fiscal*, fiscal code, that would be used to deduct taxes from my income, although I didn't know if I'd ever have any of that.

I gave Rocco a hug. "I don't know how to thank you," I said.

"I think you will like to see me tonight," he said.

When he picked me up later in his SUV, he handed me a pink rose. Finally, he was being romantic. We drove to a quiet area by a lake in the Roman countryside, with lovely views of the city in the distance.

He took my hand and kissed it. He told me he was drawn to me because of my truthfulness. "You say what you think. I like that," he said. We began to kiss.

From there, it was the same old story, as ancient as the hills: Girl meets boy. Boy helps girl with tax card and gives her a pink rose. Girl is made to feel extremely special after spending so much time agonizing over her life's choices. Girl and boy move from kissing in the front seat to having sex in the cramped back seat of boy's car.

And then, the capper, also as ancient as the hills and just as tired: As I was pulling my sweater back down over my head, Rocco, already acting distant, said: "I need to tell you something. I have an ex-girlfriend, a top model. She left me a few months ago, but recently she told me she wants me back."

I had no idea how to respond. He hadn't held me or cuddled after sex, so I felt as if suddenly we were having a different conversation that had nothing to do with me, even though it had everything to do with me. "Are you thinking of going back with her?" I asked, which seemed like the only polite thing to say under these odd circumstances.

"I don't think so."

"Oh," I said, confused but a little happier.

"But, well, I also see another woman."

"Oh," I said, distinctly unhappy now.

"She is married. I see her for ... relations."

"I see."

I did *not* see. I felt anesthetized, unable to move, unable to respond, not knowing what to say in any case. My mother had taught me to send thank-you notes for gifts, but no one had told me what to do in situations where the moment a guy zips his pants back up he announces a laundry list of women who are ahead of me in line.

As he drove me back to the Residence, Rocco hummed an Italian love song. He was happy, while I felt like crying. What had this evening been about? Was it really just the tax card, a kind of sordid quid pro quo? Had Rocco meant all the nice things he said to me earlier or was that just a script he'd been following, one he always trotted out whenever there was moonglow and a lake view?

"I will call you tomorrow, darlin'," he said as he dropped me off. Sometimes he left off the hard "g" at the end of a word to sound carefree and almost Texan.

That night I took a tranquilizer to help me fall asleep.

I confided everything about Rocco to my Italian teacher, whom I was seeing twice a week for lessons. Confiding to her about my love life, or lack of one, was another way of practicing my Italian.

"I am here for you," Flavia said, enveloping me in a warm hug. "You are like a daughter to me, and you deserve to be happy."

Just because a woman acted motherly toward me didn't totally save me from those nagging, lifelong feelings of isolation and confusion. In a way, my new life in Rome didn't feel so much different from how I felt as a little girl, needy and dependent, wondering where I belonged in the world.

I took some solace in a new friendship with Nancy, the woman I had met on the plane. She called out of the blue one day and asked me to lunch, and we went to her favorite restaurant, near Piazza Navona, a short walk from the Residence. There we each had a huge plate of grilled vegetables with bread, and then strolled around Piazza Navona, Trevi Fountain, Via del Corso, and finally back to the Residence through Villa Borghese. By the time I got back, it was already 5 o'clock. Nancy had taken my mind off my concerns—work, money, Rocco—but my loneliness trailed me home and caught up with me at the door of my studio.

Why hadn't I waited to know more about Rocco before I went tumbling into bed with him, or into the back seat of his SUV?

I didn't know what I would do over the next few hours. More Italian homework? More TV? More biscotti? The gym was only open for half-days on Sundays, and sometimes they'd be closed that day for no reason. Sundays often felt like pure loneliness. That day had always been tough for me, maybe because my mother had always been at her moodiest on Sundays when I was a child. I was Pavlov's dog, except without the promise of a treat. I'd been conditioned to expect the worst on the last day of the week.

The phone rang. It was Rocco, wanting to come over.

Oh, happy day! Oh, happy Sunday! I flew around the studio, neatening, straightening. I showered *again*. I donned a low-cut yet classy blouse, and nice underwear.

Rocco had asked what kind of pizza I liked, "*con funghi o peperoni o normale,*" and I had chosen plain. He said his friend Angelo, the one who had sat like a silent chaperone on our first date, made the best pizza in town, and he would bring one. At last, Angelo was serving a purpose in this relationship.

Was it a relationship? Would it ever be one? If Rocco wanted to see me again so soon, did this mean I had won out over the top model and the married sex goddess?

When he arrived at my door, I put my arms around his shoulders and gave him a big hug, even though I wasn't sure what I was or should be feeling about him. He gave me a quick kiss on the mouth and revealed what was in the cardboard box he carried: Luigi had fashioned for us a heart-shaped pizza.

"Oh my God!" I cried. "That is extraordinary. And did you know that my middle name is Valentine?" (This is true!)

We held a long kiss even though, oddly, Rocco's mouth was tightly closed.

We laughed during dinner, and the conversation flowed easily. He held my hand while awkwardly trying to eat his slice of pizza with the other. I had even more trouble because I was self-conscious of any oil or tomato left on my lips after a bite.

After dinner, we lay down on my bed. "I need to be careful now," said Rocco. "I don't want to get hurt."

"I understand completely. I'm the same way," I said. "That's why I can't have sex with you if you are going to sleep with anyone else."

"Look at me," he said. I moved closer to him. "I am not going to be with anyone else."

"Really? Do you mean that?"

"Of course."

We made love that night, and even though Rocco left at midnight, and even though I awoke in the morning to the steady drip, drip, drip of all my hotel room's faucets leaking, I felt very happy.

10

For weeks, I tried to get back in touch with the producer, Gianmarco, to tell him it would not be possible for me to move to Milan at this time. The woman who answered his phone would always tell me he was not there but that she would deliver the message that I'd called.

Maybe I didn't need Gianmarco after all. Suddenly, I was getting names of agents from many different quarters. Manuel, the trainer at the Roman Sports Center, said that I should speak to Riccardo, another member of the gym, whose office was within walking distance. For once, it was an address that I could easily find.

Riccardo was tall, slim, and balding, but with long sideburns. He smelled strongly of sweet cologne.

When he looked at me and then at my resumé, he said, "Ahhh, you are a good type."

I didn't know what "a good type" was, but it sounded positive. Was it because I was similar to the Italian actresses, or because I was so different from them? I had been considered a "good type" back in New York, too, but apparently never good enough to get into the Screen Actors Guild. It meant I'd had to take a lot of exhausting, low-paid work as an extra, hoping I'd get noticed by a director or one of the union producers and get "upgraded" to a real part, but all that happened was that I had to eat dinner with the other non-union actors at midnight in a separate area, cordoned off from the union people.

I got another name of an agent through someone else I had met in Rome, another friend-of-a-friend-of-etc. I met with this agent, Christo, who asked me to bring headshots and my resumé. I had brought to Italy half a suitcase full of both those, knowing I would need them.

Christo looked directly at me with an approving gaze. "You are a good type," he said. "You look European or Italian with your dark hair and eyes, and you can also look American, and you're pretty, so I think I can use you."

I was thrilled. "Do you have anything I can audition for right now?" I asked, hoping against hope.

"I will send you to Shaila Rubin, an American casting director. She is casting some small parts right now for a film at *Cinecittà*."

I knew of that studio. Everyone did. It was quite famous, the place where all the spaghetti westerns had been shot, and home over the years to directors from Coppola and Scorsese to Fellini, Bertolucci, and Visconti. Dozens of the films shot there had gone on to win Oscars.

I was so excited I could barely breathe. "What are they shooting?" I asked, trying to contain myself.

"It is a film called *Daylight*," he said. "The star is Sylvester Stallone."

Was he kidding? Was this a dream? Stallone was A-list! Stallone was Rocky and Rambo!

It did strike me as funny that I had to move all the way to Italy to make it into a major American movie, and I had a moment of panic that the agent would assume I knew how to do my own stunts, or that I had Rambo-like abilities that would qualify me for being in an action movie. Did I need to have zero-body-fat the way Stallone did? I was in fairly good shape, but I might have to reconsider those six nightly biscotti.

I had to fold my street map all the way out to find Shaila Rubin's apartment in the heart of Rome. Even so, I had to stop multiple times and ask for directions. It's true that I am terrible with directions, but I have to say in my own defense that Rome is not an easy city to maneuver.

Sheila was a tiny woman, originally from New Jersey, who had studied the violin and viola before getting involved in movies and moving to Rome. She smoked non-stop and had a smoker's cough. She took my headshots and said she would call me.

I skipped out of there like a schoolgirl. I was going to have a part in an American action movie! How cool was that?

It did seem that my luck was changing. Even though the economy was bad and even Italian actors were having trouble finding work, Riccardo, the agent who worked out at my gym, thought I was a good type for *pubblicità*, TV commercials, and set me up for an ad for mozzarella cheese.

I immediately made an appointment with a hairdresser, so I would look as good (and Italian) as possible. "You can dress casually," Riccardo told me. "Wear a skirt and a nice shirt."

I went through my closet and chose a black, form-fitted skirt and a pink blouse. On camera, those colors looked good on me.

My experience in New York was that for commercials, they usually wanted a particular look—a thirtysomething neurotic type like the Elaine Bennis character from *Seinfeld*, for example. Or a sexy car saleswoman with a low-cut blouse. Often there was copy to read or try to memorize quickly, but I wouldn't know until I got there.

At ten the next morning I was en route to the casting director's office, my head held high. Here I was in Rome on my way to my first audition!

At the casting director's office, I sat in the last available seat. All the other actresses had short skirts—mine was knee-length—and tight blouses. They had long, heavy hair that partly covered their face, while I always wore my long hair loosely tied back. Did they know something I didn't? Or was I the standout, the one who got attention for being different?

There was no script. I wondered what I would be doing for this audition aside from eating cheese. After forty-five minutes of fidgeting and adjusting my hair and applying more lipstick, the casting director, unshaven and with a big toothy grin, called my name.

"*Buon giorno*," I said inside the audition room. There was a single camera and a table with a big plate of cheese. It was a good thing I was not lactose intolerant.

"Eat the cheese and look directly into the camera," he instructed me in Italian. "Look sensuous while you are saying *buonissimo, buonissimo.*" Very good.

Look sensuous? I was way too nervous. During the first take, I spit cheese from my mouth while trying to say *buonissimo.*

He told me to do it again. He used his hands theatrically to suggest the heights of ecstasy I should be feeling as I sampled the cheese.

I tried again. As I put the second piece of cheese in my mouth, I puckered my lips and tried to look carnal. *Buon-iss-imo.* It was just one word, but the cheese got stuck against my teeth.

I did it again. This time, as I swallowed the cheese, I bit my tongue and felt a dab of blood inside my mouth. I did not feel sensuous, and I was pretty sure I didn't look it, either.

I did five more takes before it was over. I wouldn't know for a while whether I had landed the gig, and I had probably consumed a full day's allotment of calories from fat and dairy, but I felt proud of myself. I had the interest of agents, I had gone on an audition, and I felt *fantastico.*

I didn't get the mozzarella commercial, but soon after that, Riccardo sent me on another audition. This one was for a small part in an Italian telefilm.

The audition was held in an unfamiliar part of the city—although one could argue that, to me, most of the city was unfamiliar. I walked around half an hour trying to locate the building and finally had to ask a passing priest (a really cute one; all the men in Italy are cute) for help.

None of the buildings had any numbers on them. The priest looked at the piece of paper on which I had written the address, looked up, and pointed right away to the correct building. How did he know? Some things about Italy just cannot be taught, I supposed.

Once I was where I was supposed to be, the casting director looked me over and handed me a script to read in Italian. He gave me a few minutes to focus on the words, but I couldn't shake off the terror of trying to speak Italian like a native. "*Mario, non vedo l'ora di vederti amore,*" I read from the script. "*Quando vieni a casa?*" Mario, I can't wait to see you, love. When will you come back home?

Everything in Italian film is dubbed, including the Italian actors. I had heard that even Sophia Loren was often dubbed. Dubbing actors are in high demand in that country. Even so, my Italian embarrassed me, despite my best efforts to sound fluent.

"I can use your type," said the casting agent. "You are a good type for me. *Un tipo speciale.*" I had no idea what this good, different, special type was, but I was happy to hear it.

I didn't get the part.

11

I deduced that Rocco was my boyfriend now. It wasn't because we had discussed it and agreed on the terminology, but we had been seeing each other, and he was being more attentive and romantic.

One night he offered to come over and cook dinner for me. He said he needed to tell me something.

He arrived with a grocery bag full of pasta, sauce, cheese, and a bottle of wine, but I was more interested in whatever it was he wanted to discuss with me. I hoped it was something romantic. Before he even made dinner, I pressed him on it.

"Listen," he said. "I have a gun."

I recoiled. This was certainly not what I had expected to hear. I had secretly been thinking he might say *ti amo*, I love you.

"I bring it with me all the time," he said. "I need to know if this bothers you." He took it from his pocket and laid the black, shiny revolver on the table where soon we would be eating dinner.

"But why ... why do you need a gun?" I asked. I also wondered whether it was loaded, but was too unnerved to ask.

"I need it for work. I drive through dangerous areas outside of Rome."

"What do you do for work again?"

"I transport merchandise out of Rome. Very boring to explain."

"Well, could you put the gun away for now? Put it back in your jacket?"

After Rocco made us the pasta dinner in my tiny kitchenette, he took my hand and kissed it. "I think we will fall in love," he said. "You are silent. I think you agree."

Once Rocco had gotten the gun conversation off his mind, he did get slightly more romantic. He announced that he was going to take me the following night to a restaurant filled with candles. I wore a sexy new sleeveless sheath that had a silky slip peeking out from beneath. The dress made me feel beautiful, and very Italian. Rocco, too, looked great, in a dark suit and tie. I hoped that we would reach a new level of intimacy in our relationship that evening.

After our candlelit dinner, we returned to the Residence. The first thing Rocco did was to turn on the TV. Not a good sign, I thought. I turned it off.

Rocco lay on my bed with his arms folded tightly across his chest. I often had to be the seducer with him, and I wanted him to initiate romance more often. He took off his clothes but did not try to kiss me or hug me. He just lay there.

"Can you talk more sexy to me?" he asked all of a sudden.

"You want me to talk dirty to you?" I said. "Honestly, I'm not even that comfortable doing it in English. I guess I'm a little more on the traditional side." I tried to give him a kiss instead, but his mouth was frozen shut. It only opened to emit a giant yawn before he got up and put his clothes on again.

"I will call you tomorrow, darlin'," he said.

I didn't sleep well, and woke early with *un grande mal di testa*, a big headache. There were loud voices in the garden beneath my window. The Residence often hosted gatherings of politicians and journalists, whose stale cigarette smoke wafted up through my window along with the sound of their arguments and debates.

I wandered downstairs to the lobby, which still had the ambiance of the Baroque 17th-century convent it had once been. The clientele, mostly from the arts and business worlds, often resided there for months.

I saw Andrea, an Italian staying at the Residence with whom I spoke on occasion, and went over to him. He was always chain-smoking and could never sit still.

"Allow me to introduce you to my wife, Mary Rose," he said. "She is just in from New York."

I greeted his wife, who was quite slender, with platinum-blonde hair and a touch of a New Jersey accent. As we stood there chatting, it turned out that she had been married to her Italian husband for many years and understood the Italian way of life. "You must use this place to your advantage," she advised me. "There are many important and high-caliber people who stay here: politicians, theatrical people, and just people with connections. You know what I mean."

"Thank you," I said. "But I'm so glad that *you're* here now," I added, liking the idea of having a new friend more than networking for my career.

"Just be careful with the Italians, honey," she said. "They go very fast. Madonna, *puttana*."

This was not the first time I'd heard of the "mother-whore complex" that was said to afflict Italian men, making them act worshipful in some instances with women and cavalier in others. "But you're married to an Italian," I said. "Do you really think it's such a problem?"

"Absolutely. They struggle to have an intimate relationship with a woman," she said. "This is because their mothers always do everything for them and certain men can't separate a sexual and romantic feeling for a woman from what their mother's maternal love represented."

"I'm seeing an Italian man right now, and it is a little strange with him," I said. "What should I do?"

"You must train him."

The next time Rocco came over, he brought a plain pizza margherita with cheese and tomatoes—not heart-shaped, just the normal kind. The days of heart-shaped pizzas were already behind us.

I hoped to have a discussion with him about our lack of intimacy. "I like you, I like your heart," I started. "But when you asked me to talk dirty the other night, it made me feel whorish, in a way. Like a *puttana*."

Rocco put his hands to his head and looked as if he were about to cry. "I feel ashamed," he said. "Can you explain?"

"It's just that we don't kiss or touch or hug. I cannot just have sex; I need to make love. Do you understand the difference?"

Rocco was silent, in heavy contemplation. "Maybe I don't know how to love," he finally said. "Okay, we shouldn't have sex tonight. I am in a very difficult time of my life and am confused and then I met you. Can you give me time?"

"Of course," I said. I went over to him and gave him a hug.

We lay down on the bed for a while, but our bodies were a few feet apart, facing in opposite directions. I let out a sigh of relief as we both turned simultaneously towards each other. He put his arms around my waist.

"Stay with me," I said. "Don't go." If ever there was a time to "train" Rocco, this was it.

He came closer and awkwardly caressed me like a puppet on a string, but at least he was trying. I took his head in my hands and ever so delicately touched my lips to his. As we held the kiss, I opened my lips slightly so that the kiss was not so hard. Initially, he didn't follow my lead, but gradually he relaxed his mouth. Intimacy at last!

After we made love, he stayed next to me with our arms entwined, although when he left he repeated that he needed some time.

Overall, I thought I had done well. I had managed to have "the intimacy talk" that even American men shied away from. Rocco had made a real effort and seemed to want to learn how to change.

I felt more confident. That's why I was ready when Leonardo finally called. I wasn't ready in the sense that I had my little speech at hand for telling him off. In fact, the minute I heard that familiar voice on the phone—"*Ciao Alison, come stai?*" Hello Alison, how are you?—I scrambled to find my little cheat sheet of righteous Italian phrases, and simply could not find it. I was on my own, but I made the best of it.

"*Sei incredibile,*" I said, my voice clear and controlled. "*Non mi fai una chiamata da settimane... Sono molto delusa da te.*" Leonardo, you are incredible. There wasn't one telephone call from you for weeks. I am very disappointed in you.

It was Leonardo who was left searching for words. He told me he had been busy. He told me he would call again very soon.

I didn't care. I had gotten through an important conversation *in Italian*.

After I hung up, I turned on the radio and danced around my room.

12

Riccardo, the agent from my gym, called about another audition, but sounded in a hurry and didn't tell me anything about it.

"What is this for?" I asked.

"*Un provo*," an audition. "Just go and look good. There is no copy to read in Italian."

The first thing the casting director did after I arrived at her office and signed in was to direct me to pick up the copy on the table and study it.

"Copy?" I said, immediately panicked.

"*Si è sulla tavola.*" Yes, here on the table.

The piece of paper contained words filling up more than half the page. I went to the ladies' room to splash cold water on my face. My hands were trembling, and I was starting to hyperventilate.

In the waiting room, dozens of Italian women auditioning for the same part were practicing the lines, speaking them out loud without a care in the world. I had ten minutes to prepare. I couldn't concentrate. Whatever self-confidence I'd had when I walked in had walked out without saying good-bye. I was wet lettuce in a salad spinner.

"Alessandra Rand." They were calling my name, in Italian. In a language I couldn't speak, let alone correct them in. *"Per favore può leggere il copione e guardare la telecamera."* Something about a camera. They wanted me to read the copy into the camera. I had no idea what the words meant and wasn't even sure what product I was trying to sell. I stumbled through it, hating every second, and hating myself.

"Okay, *signorina, può lasciare*." It is okay to leave the room.

She called the next name on her list.

I had always been somewhat naïve about what it meant to be an actress. Part of this was because other people, too, have odd ideas about the profession.

In New York, I often got patronizing looks after explaining that I wasn't an actress in the theater, but in mostly TV commercials. They didn't consider that "real" acting, not realizing that many, if not most, actors start out this way—taking whatever they can get, for the money, experience, and exposure, no matter how lofty their ultimate ambitions.

Personally, I did not at all mind staying in commercials, but since everyone else seemed to think it was sub-par work, it was difficult to maintain a high level of self-esteem about it. However, when I was able to book a commercial out of a field of 500 other actresses, I'd get a shot of pleasure (as well as income) that kept me focused on the next win. It was a competitive business, no matter what anyone thought of the artistic standards of TV ads, and it was hard work to be the only one chosen. Was I playing out my childhood trauma of needing to come first in someone's life? I don't know, and it didn't matter. I enjoyed the work and, when I wasn't melting down and flubbing the audition like I had just done, I was good at it.

Mary Rose, the wife of my friend Andrea at the hotel, had said something one day that left me taken aback. "You know, honey," she said, "to be an actress in Italy you have to fuck around. I know the way it works here."

I could never be an actress who slept around for work, and I'm not sure I believed Mary Rose. People said that all the time in the States, too. They said it knowingly even if they weren't actors themselves, as if it had to be true, but I had never done such a thing in New York, and I wasn't about to do that in Rome.

Nevertheless, what she had said upset me. Maybe she *did* know the system here better than I. Maybe it wasn't my language skills that were lacking, but something else.

Still feeling lousy after bombing the audition, I asked at the gym for a referral to an acting teacher. It wouldn't hurt to keep studying, to keep learning, to at least hone my craft.

I got in touch with Carol, an American acting teacher who lived in Trastevere, considered the Greenwich Village of Rome. We set up a time for me to check out her acting class, to see if it was right for me. I walked there along the Tiber, daydreaming about all the work I would get once I was better trained, more fluent, and the right "type" for the right casting agent.

With the river on my left, the tall trees bending toward it, I passed Castel Sant' Angelo and, ten minutes later, the Vatican. I didn't need my city map for once. This time I knew where I was going.

Carol was a strong-willed American expatriate who had lived in Rome for over 30 years. She was also a dubbing actress, and when she heard my speaking voice, she recommended that we have a session or two together so that I could audition for dubbing work through one of her contacts. Maybe there was another way to work here in Rome after all.

Carol's acting class couldn't have come at a better time. It had been a fatiguing week, and I was feeling lonely and tired.

Her class was fine, but its value to me was more that it felt like another safe place to go, like the gym. It was a mix of Italians and Americans, and just being there gave me a feeling of calmness. It felt like being in a community of like-minded people, a mini-family for the person whose family had broken apart so early in life. Carol had us read different scenes and pick scene partners to work with in between classes. The whole enterprise felt therapeutic.

Carol also kept her promise to hook me up with dubbing opportunities. She sent me to Frank, the dubbing boss at American Recording Artists. He invited me to come into the studio and observe the process first-hand. "Give me a call next week, and we'll make an appointment," he said.

I was glad I had a little time before I met with him. I wanted to make a perfect impression, but I wasn't feeling well.

The Italians say they "take" a coffee or a tea. They also say they "take" a cold, and I had taken a bad one. *Ho preso un grande raffredore.*

With all the stress of moving to Rome, it was a miracle I hadn't gotten ill before. But now, I was feeling quite sick, with a painful cough and a fever. I hadn't canceled my Italian lesson with Flavia, but when I got out of bed to get dressed and turned on the faucet in the bathroom, there was no hot water. The icy-cold shower I took didn't do much to help my cold.

Flavia told me again that I was very *brava*, good. That I was doing great and speaking well, even if I didn't feel well. I didn't quite believe her, but it was good to hear nevertheless.

I was now trusting myself to simply speak without worrying about mistakes or sounding stupid. That was the best lesson I ever learned from Flavia.

After the lesson I went back to bed, hacking away. I called Rocco, hoping for some emotional support as well as a referral to a doctor, but he cut me off short, saying he couldn't talk right then and that he would call back. Whatever progress he'd made since our discussion of intimacy seemed to disappear at times in a puff of smoke.

After I had used up my one complimentary box of Residence tissues, I went downstairs to ask the concierge for another box. As I was waiting for him to retrieve it from the storage room, I noticed a familiar face over by the bar—the American character actor Martin Balsam.

"Are you...?" I asked.

"Yes, dear," he said with a smile.

He was also living at the Residence. "I love it here in Rome," he told me. "It's my favorite place in the world."

Mary Rose had mentioned that he was living here. She said he was looking unwell and feeble, but he was around 76 years old at the time, and after a career that went all the way back to *Psycho* and *12 Angry Men*, I thought it was only natural that he should look a little careworn.

I felt a little star-struck around him. It made me feel better, despite my fears of being sick and alone, to know that the Residence was his home, too.

The concierge gave me more than just tissues. He also got me an appointment for the next afternoon with "the doctor to the stars," as he put it.

I walked to the doctor's office because getting a taxi in Rome was no easy feat. His office was near the American Embassy on the Via Veneto, about a half hour walk that normally would have been fine, but which today left me huffing and puffing, wheezing and coughing.

"What is wrong, young lady?" asked Dr. Stessi.

"I feel awful," I said. "And I have a bad cough."

While he listened to my breathing, he asked what I was doing in Rome. I told him about looking for acting work there.

"You have a bad case of bronchitis," he told me and wrote down two things on his prescription pad. One was an Rx for antibiotics, twice as strong as what was doled out in the U.S. The other was the name of a producer friend of his. "I'll call him first on your behalf," he said

I couldn't believe it. Another little miracle here in Rome, worthy of consideration from the Vatican. One minute I was so down I was like a dog being punished for nibbling its owner's shoes, and the next minute, despite a non-stop deep cough, the phone was ringing the minute I returned to the Residence. It was a call from Dr. Stessi, saying that it was all clear—not my bronchial condition, of course, but that it was okay to contact his producer friend.

I reached *Michele*, the producer, right after I got off with Dr. Stessi. We were even able to converse in English.

"Tell me, how old are you?" he asked.

"32," I said, although I was 37. It wasn't a complete lie because many people agreed that I *looked* 32.

"That is a good age for work here," he said. "There is a big-budget film coming to Rome in September. I'll call you tomorrow, and we can meet."

Al destino non si comanda. When it rains, it pours.

The next evening, after taking my cough medicine and antibiotics, I was trying to make sense of the subjunctive tense for my Italian homework when the phone rang. It was nearly 10:00 p.m., so I assumed it was Rocco.

It was Michele, the producer friend of the doctor to the stars.

"I would like to come over in half an hour to meet you," he said.

Really? This late? It didn't feel right. Plus, I was busy hacking away.

"*Beh, invece di stasera potremmo vederci domani sera, con un po' di preavviso,*" I said. Well, instead of tonight we could meet tomorrow, with a little advance notice.

"*Non lo so. Ti chiamerò domani.*" I don't know. I will call you tomorrow.

That was probably stupid of me. *Che stupido.* But all I could hear was Mary Rose's voice, about how in Italy the only way to get a role was to trade sexual favors for it.

I didn't think that producer would ever call again, but soon enough it didn't matter.

"*Pronto?*" Ready? I said, answering the phone the next day at a decent hour.

It was Shaila Rubin, the casting agent. My heart thumped so loudly I could barely hear what she had to say.

"Are you free next week to come in for a screen test?" she asked. "We're casting the Stallone film."

13

Feverish with excitement, I needed to diffuse my anxiety, so I walked at a quick pace to Shaila's apartment where she was casting the smaller parts for the Stallone film.

A British girl, Janie, handed me the script, and I quickly studied the few lines I would have to read on camera. The part was small, but I didn't mind. It was a real part in an actual Sylvester Stallone movie!

The premise of *Daylight* was that a collision between a truck carrying illegal toxic waste and a truck carrying smuggled diamonds sets off a fireball inside the Holland Tunnel connecting Manhattan to New Jersey. With both tunnel entrances caved in and the water rising at a rapid rate, the only person who can rescue the few survivors inside is none other than Stallone—playing a disgraced former Emergency Medical Services chief who is now a cab driver. The characters are always about to get blown up, drowned, or suffocated, but Stallone perseveres and only loses a few of them on the way to the big finale.

I was not reading for the part of a tunnel motorist whose face gets melted off in the fireball. The part I was reading was for one of the control people from the Port Authority of New York and New Jersey.

"Are you ready?" Janie said. "Okay, go."

"Captain, there's been an explosion inside the tunnel. We are trying to get people out."

"Good," said Janie. "Now again, and do the next few lines too."

"The same way?" I asked.

"A little more urgency."

I firmed up my voice and tried to speak with more insistence. "CAPTAIN!" I bellowed. "There's been an EXPLOSION inside the TUNNEL! We're trying to get people out, but it's a TOXIC FIRE! There must be HUNDREDS trapped inside." A beat of silence. "*I'm on it, Captain!*"

"Really good," Janie said.

"Is that it?" I asked.

"You did well."

She was already calling in the next girl. Now it was up to fate, and to the casting gods.

In truth, I'd had successive careers that hadn't worked out so well. I was hoping that acting would be different.

When I was 20, I left college after two years to become a flight attendant for American Airlines. I hoped the job would be a good way to meet people from all over the country and would help me learn about dealing with the public. Plus, I have to admit that I thought that with constant traveling I would somehow be able to outrun my loneliness.

I did everything the airline asked of me. I chopped my long lovely chestnut hair down to chin length. I wore the blue polyester uniform. I kept my weight down, although they insisted on checking it at humiliating periodic weigh-ins. To them, I should weigh no more than 130 pounds. But at 5-foot-7, I sometimes edged up to 132. I blamed it on having to eat in pitch blackness at 4:00 a.m. for some of my shifts, or on helping myself to the airline chicken Kiev after serving the first-class passengers. On one of the surprise weigh-ins, while I was still in my six-month probationary period, I got the earth-shattering news that I was three pounds over their limit. "I'll do better next time," I promised.

There was no next time.

I also had a brief flirtation with a career in advertising. Landing a job as a junior copywriter was a big deal since it was hard to break into that field. My father was in advertising, so I felt it must run in the blood.

I called my brother to share with him the good news.

"I just got hired as a junior copywriter for sports ads," I said.

"That's great, little one," said David. "So you're into sports now," he added with a chuckle.

"Well, no," I admitted. "Frankly, I'm a little stressed about it."

"Don't worry, I'll teach you the lingo. You'll be great!"

I tried to look the part of a creative person. I wore my hair big and layered. My lack of enthusiasm for sports, though, was an issue, and the job barely lasted more than a year.

There were certainly people I knew who didn't think I should take up acting. Their objections were reasonable—that it was a tough profession to crack, that most working actors barely scraped by, that actresses, in particular, had a short shelf life. One thing about me, though, despite all my fears and anxiety, is that I am determined and resilient. I never turn my back on something just because it might be difficult.

Now all that seemed to be paying off. I was living in Rome and had two agents, plus the possibility of a role in a Sylvester Stallone movie.

Hope and despair were my two constant emotions, but right now hope was winning out. After breakfast, I walked to the Italian *questura*, police station, to pick up my first *permesso di soggiorno*. Having that document would mean I was legally allowed to stay in Italy for three months. I had gone there a few weeks prior to fill out the form and attach my photo, and now I was going to pick it up.

When I got there, a policewoman told me in Italian to come back between 1:00 and 2:00 p.m. Piece of cake. In a few hours I would be legal in Italy for three more months, and by then I hoped to have figured out how to get a more permanent *permesso*. When I returned that afternoon, the policewoman handed me my document, and I practically danced home.

Once in my room, I looked at the paper more closely. The *permesso* was good for only one more week. They had started the three-month clock on the day I had actually arrived in Italy, May 1, so it was set to expire on August 1, which was very soon.

It had to be a mistake, a clerical error. I had done everything the way I was supposed to, so this couldn't be right.

The next morning I returned to the *questura*. The policewoman I had spoken to wasn't there, so I spoke to someone else. "*Mi scusi, ma c'è un errore. La data non è corretto*," I said in my finest Italian. There is an error. The date is not correct.

The policeman barely looked at me as he stubbed out his cigarette and looked at my document. He told me in Italian that the date was correct, and that I needed a visa to get a *permesso* for more than three months. The *permesso* I had received was for tourists, *turismo*; not for living there, *soggiorno*.

I tried to ask more questions, but he had already moved on to the next person. However, since I am a person who does not give up, I returned the following day and tried again. I needed to get my life to work for me in Rome. I also needed more time to "train" Rocco so that he would be a better boyfriend.

On this visit, I was told that I had to go to the Italian consulate in New York to inquire about getting a visa so I could stay longer than three months and eventually get a *permesso di lavoro*, a work permit. So many *permessos*, so little time.

Going back to New York just to get a piece of paper to allow me to stay in Italy seemed ridiculous, not to mention expensive. But if that's how things worked here, I was prepared to follow the rules. Otherwise, I wouldn't be able to work on the Stallone film, if that came through.

I was starting to fret about money. I didn't spend lavishly and had enough to see me through six months in Rome, but I had used up nearly half that time already and still hadn't made enough to sustain me should I decide to stay overseas permanently.

Worry here had a different feeling from worrying back in New York because here, there was always a sudden opportunity to hang out with a big, boisterous crowd of new friends. It helped make all my problems seem like occasional intrusions on the bigger party of life. So, just when I was starting to count my *lire*, my friend Luigi called to invite me on Sunday to the beach at Frigene, along with some of his pals.

Frigene is a town on the Tyrrhenian coast whose heyday was in the 1960s and '70s when it was favored by artists, writers, and filmmakers. It was still popular with young people as a getaway from the noise and blur of the city.

I was glad the outing was for a Sunday, my toughest day in terms of keeping it together. I even boasted about it to Rocco, trying to rouse a spark of jealousy in him, or a spark of anything. Ever since my experiment in "training" him, he had become inaccessible. "Have a good day," was all he said about Frigene. He didn't even ask who was taking me there.

It did not seem as if I had a boyfriend after all. Which is why my eye began to wander that Sunday, finally settling on Alberto—a striking, dark-haired friend of Luigi with movie-star looks. He pulled up in his car to get me, with Luigi and another friend, Simona, in the back seat. Alberto spoke a little English, but I tried to keep the conversation going in Italian, for practice.

"*Ciao, piacere,*" he said with a bright smile. Hi, it's a pleasure.

"*Piacere. Dov'e'...*" I was going to ask where I should sit.

"*Vieni a sederti vicino a me.*" Next to him.

At the beach, we changed in separate men's and women's bathhouses into our bathing suits and then plopped onto lounge chairs, slathered in suntan oil. The sand was a soft, deep beige. It was perfect.

"I'm going into the water," I announced. "Is anyone joining me?"

"You cannot go in," Simona said. She pointed to some signs a slight distance away: *Non entrare in acqua. E' inquinata.* Do not enter the water. It's polluted. "Better to just look from a distance," she said with a laugh.

Luigi played the clown, as usual—making silly gestures and pretending to flex his not very muscular biceps—but Alberto in his sunglasses and laid-back manner seemed much more charming and attractive. I overheard him mention my name when he was speaking quickly in Italian to the others.

"What did he say about me?" I asked Simona, pulling her aside.

"*Cara, ha detto che sei molto affascinante. Sei bella e intelligente.*"

He had said I was very charming and pretty and intelligent. I couldn't wait to see him again.

14

I had my chance to see Alberto again soon enough. The following week, Luigi invited me to a party at Alberto's house.

The party started late, naturally, so I prepared by taking my *pisolino*, nap. Luigi picked me up.

Alberto looked just as gorgeous as he did at the beach, only without his sunglasses I could see his soulful, intelligent brown eyes. He was also a great cook, it turned out. He had made the entire feast himself, laid out on a long table: baked chicken, pasta, vegetables, and salad. There was a separate dessert area with cookies and slices of fruit.

There were about fifteen other guests. After dinner, they made a line to dance the Macarena. Around midnight, Alberto drove me home, and when he parked in front of the Residence, he kissed me.

It wasn't like Rocco, with that sealed, grim mouth. Alberto was a skilled kisser; it was thrilling to make out with him.

I called Simona the next morning to ask her what she thought.

"*Si, Alison, secondo me gli piaci ma ... penso che lui abbia una ragazza.*" Yes, I think he likes you, but I think he has a girlfriend.

They all had girlfriends. Every man I met seemed to have one, if not more. Just hearing the word *ragazza* was starting to make my stomach clench. Why, if he had a *ragazza*, did he kiss me like he had?

I wanted to see Alberto again, to understand whether he was really interested in me.

When he called a few days later to invite me to another party, I eagerly accepted, but when my phone rang at 10:00 p.m. on the appointed night, it was Alberto's brother, Luca.

"I come to take you to party in ten minute," he said in halting English. I knew that ten minutes meant more like thirty, but I was eager to once again see Alberto, *il grande baciatore*, the great kisser.

Luca was very polite when he picked me up. He got out of the car to open the door for me and tried very hard to make conversation in English.

Luigi was at the party and had brought two more women with him. Simona from the beach was there with her husband, Gabrielle. They were all glued to the TV screen watching *Scent of a Woman* with Al Pacino dubbed into Italian, blasting at full volume. You haven't lived until you've heard Al Pacino yell "HOO-ah" with an Italian accent.

"Does anyone want to go get ice cream?" asked Alberto unexpectedly when it was already after eleven, way past my bedtime.

"*Si, Si*," I said, seeing this as an opportunity to get away from the blasting TV, and to possibly be alone with Alberto.

After a dish of rich, perfectly flavored gelato, Alberto drove me home. Once again we kissed for an hour outside the door of the Residence, but I had to stop him at a certain point. My mouth and chin were getting sore from beard burn.

"I have a girlfriend in Pisa, but I would like to see you also," he told me.

"Then you're not serious with her?" I asked. "You have special feelings for me?"

"*Forse*, maybe," he said. "Only through time will we know. I will make a choice *dopo*," later.

While Alberto was off making his big decision, I thought I'd make sure that Rocco was definitely no longer interested. We had been out of touch, but only a few weeks earlier he had expressed an interest in meeting my mother and stepfather when they came to visit, and they were due in Rome in a week, so I called Rocco and asked whether he still wanted to join us for dinner.

To my surprise, he said yes.

I was nervous about everyone meeting each other. I didn't know where I stood with Rocco, and I didn't know how my mother would react to him.

We were to meet at a restaurant near the Residence. Unfortunately, Rocco showed up late and made things worse by acting cocky and arrogant. "I parked my Corvette over there," he said, before acknowledging my mother and stepfather. Over dinner, he barely asked them anything and talked mostly about himself. It wasn't hard to read my mother's body language: She hated him.

"Honey, I just think he's a bit full of himself," she told me, trying to soften the blow. "I know you can do better."

With my mom and George with me in Rome, I felt more confident in every way. At our last dinner together I ordered for everyone in Italian and chatted with the waiter as if I'd been speaking the language for years.

"Look at you," said my mother, beaming. "You're already fluent!"

"I guess I'm doing okay," I conceded with false modesty, eating up the flattery.

If Rocco wasn't going to work out, and if Alberto was taking his time deciding among his options, I figured I would be more proactive about my love life. I got in touch with Hugo, the cute, boyish son of the owner of one of the elegant mountain hotels where I'd stayed during my hiking trip in the Dolomites. Hugo had seen me at my worst—sweaty and tired after a long day of hiking, my hair tucked up under a baseball cap—and still, there had been an obvious attraction. "You have beautiful hands," he had told me when he sat with me at the bar one night after I had dinner with my group. He had taken my right hand and kissed it. He had shown me around the hotel, and we had ended up kissing on a couch in a back room.

Hugo had called me several times in New York, including on Christmas Eve. Now it was my turn to call him.

"Alison, it is so good to hear from you!" he said in his almost perfect English. He invited me to come stay at his hotel for five days the following week. "I will pick you up at the station."

The nine and a half hours by Italian Rail to Bolzano were sometimes leisurely, sometimes like a roller coaster as the train took hairpin turns along the mountains. The thought of seeing Hugo again kept me steady. I practically leapt into his arms on the platform, but my welcoming kiss landed on his cheek instead of his lips as he turns his head at the last minute.

This was not a good sign.

"I'll get the car," he said.

In the entire five days I was there, Hugo and I only spoke together a total of one and a half hours. I had no idea why he was avoiding me after he had gone out of his way to invite me in the first place. Had I done something wrong? Looked too happy to see him at the train station?

I had a panic attack while hiking on the mountain with a surly guide named Helmut. I hadn't been focusing on the beauty of the mountains, but on Hugo and this strangely disappointing getaway. Suddenly I felt I couldn't breathe.

"Just relax," said Helmut. He had a hard, unattractive, lined face. "Take some deep breaths."

"I can't get enough oxygen! I think I'm going to faint!"

Helmut sat down next to me on a rock and talked me through some breathing exercises. "I think you have a problem with your legs," he said once my breathing was back to normal. "Not muscular enough. They are too fat."

Now I was panicky *and* mortified. I wasn't good enough for Hugo, and I wasn't even good enough for a mean, aloof mountain guide. I ate dinner alone each night in the hotel dining room making awkward small talk with the waiters who were my only company, the only ones who would smile at me, even though they were paid for it.

On my last evening, I ran into Hugo near the *ingresso*, the front entrance to the lobby. "I don't understand what's going on with you," I said.

"Nothing," he said.

"I came all the way from Rome. You asked me to come."

"I met a girl who lives in Germany, and I really like her," he said. "I just want to be friends now."

Hugo picked up the tab for my entire hotel stay. He had an odd notion of what it meant to be "just friends."

I couldn't wait to get back to my studio in Rome, but as bad as my stay in the Dolomites was, the trip home was worse. It took over twelve hours, and I started out in a packed car without air conditioning where masses of people were lying on the floor. It felt as if it were WWII and we were fleeing the country.

The heat was staggering. My panic was rising. I couldn't get my bag through the hordes of people to locate my correct cabin. I began crying in frustration and left my bag behind so I could walk through seven cars to my assigned seat. That, in itself, was a miracle, but this cabin also lacked air conditioning, and the windows were locked.

I put my hand on my throat to signal that I was finding it hard to breathe, and a kindly Swiss man explained that the A/C was on a cycle that was currently off, and that the crowds were the result of a train *sciopero*, strike. At least now I could understand the cause of my misery, unlike the situation with Hugo, where I didn't understand it at all.

I arrived in Rome after midnight—dripping, disheveled, hungry. Everything was closed. When I got back to the Residence, the A/C was off for the evening.

The next time I ran into Mary Rose, I told her of my travails, and she told me it was time I looked for my own apartment.

"Honey, it's okay to feel alone, and okay to travel alone," she said. "But it's time you had a place of your own. It will add to a feeling of belonging."

I knew she was right.

15

To see some apartments, I had to ride with the real estate agent on the back of his motorino. Petrified, with traffic coming at us from every direction, I put my arms around his waist and closed my eyes.

We saw two apartments near the Pantheon. The first had a tall, narrow, creaky staircase to get to the bathroom. As someone who frequently wakes up to pee, I knew that wasn't going to work. The second was a bright, clean, spacious apartment that I liked, but I didn't want to live that close to the Pantheon—or, more to the point, that far from where I was used to living, near Piazza del Popolo.

We looked at apartments again the following week. There was one across the river in an area called Pratti—a bright, sunny apartment with a big modern kitchen. There were large windows with shutters that I could actually close without jamming my fingers. Pratti was a new area for me, a little out of my comfort zone, but the realtor said it was safe, and convenient to buses.

I signed a one-year lease.

I had worries, of course. I worried about whether my new friends Simona and Luigi would keep up with me after I moved away. I worried about whether I would hear from Rocco or Alberto. And what if I never got the *permesso di soggiorno* that I needed in order to stay in Italy longer than three months? Would I get the part in the Stallone film? Would I always have to do everything alone, forever?

There was no going back. Once I told the Residence of my plans, they booked my room for the next three months. The staff wished me well, but in their eyes, I was already out the door.

When I arrived at my new building, the *portiere*, Nelson, greeted me with a toothless, hesitant smile. "*Signorina. C'era una perdita nel bagno e il soffitto è un po' rotto.*" There was a leak in the bathroom ceiling that was flooding.

He also told me that the toilet hadn't worked since Friday. Today was a Monday, and the plumber wasn't due for another couple of days. He advised me to fill buckets of water to help flush the toilet in the meantime.

Also, there was no hot water, and the washing machine was out of order.

It was too late to return to the Residence; someone else was already living peaceably in my old room. I responded to the porter with something that alarmed both of us: I let out a shriek, like a wild animal.

I waited until a decent hour to call my mom in Florida. "I'm crazy upset," I wailed to her. "Everything here is broken, I have no bathroom, no hot water. and a leak…"

"Honey, calm down," she said.

"And no toilet!"

She told me to keep trying to find a plumber who could come earlier. Instead, I called Rocco. He didn't pick up. Then I tried Luigi. He offered to take me to dinner, which was nice of him, but I needed a plumber or a place to stay.

The apartment had been rented to me empty of furniture, and as I walked around it barefoot, I suddenly noticed that the soles of my feet were black, as if I'd been walking on coal. My new home was broken and dirty. The people I considered my "safety nets" in Rome weren't coming through.

I did the only thing I could do under these circumstances. I took a *pisolino*, a nap.

When I woke from my nap an hour later, on the pathetic mattress my landlord had supplied for me, I was firm in my mind: I had to find a different apartment. I called Francesca, the woman I had met for lunch early on and who had shown me a better way to the gym. She knew of a psychiatrist, Camilla, who wanted to rent out her apartment on the other side of the Tiber, very close to the Residence. I thought that if it didn't work out, at least I'd know a shrink in town. I couldn't tell which I needed more.

Camilla's apartment was *buio*, dark, remarkably so, like a bat cave. It had large windows with heavy wooden shutters that let in little light even when open. They faced a street along the river called Passeggiatta di Ripetta that was dim and isolated.

The furniture, too, was off-putting—each piece uncomfortable to use and as inflexible as a block of ice. Nevertheless, it had hot and cold running water, a toilet, and a shower that worked. I told Camilla I would take it.

The owner of the first apartment agreed to let me out of my lease, as long as she could keep my two-month security deposit. She also charged me the first month's phone and gas bill. It was worth it to be rid of that place, although my money anxieties were mounting. I needed to book a job soon.

I was called for another audition. I didn't know what they were selling, but I knew I wouldn't get the job the minute I walked into the casting director's office. All the other women who were trying out for the ad were a completely different type—big hair, low-cut blouses, and short skirts. I had worn a tailored skirt and a buttoned-down blouse. I looked as conservative as a nun.

The casting director barely spoke English, so it was difficult for me to follow her directions as she told me to pick up the biscuit, taste it, and show how good it was with my eyes and my mouth. My eyes were probably full of fear, and my mouth was puckered from lack of saliva. I was parched.

"Yummm," I said while trying to chew the hard, dry biscuit.

"*Potrebbe provare di nuovo.*" Do it again.

I tried, but it took me ten seconds to swallow the biscuit before the "yummm." They were already on to the next girl.

I really had to book a job soon. Right now, my expenses were going straight onto my AmEx card, and the bill was being sent to my mother in Florida, but I would have to take over those payments eventually and pay her back, too.

I went to the bank, Banca di Lavoro, to withdraw some more cash. The ATM ate my card and wouldn't spit it back out. I nearly had another panic attack right there on the street.

I went inside and asked for the manager. "*Parla inglese?*" Fortunately, he did speak a little English. "My bank card is stuck in the machine!" I blurted out.

He called a few people on the telephone, and then, somehow, the ATM opened its jaws and released my card. "*Signorina*, this was just an error," he told me.

"Oh, okay. An error. Thank you," I said, coming down from the heights of anxiety.

Later that afternoon, after lunch, I returned to the bank, which smelled like an ashtray and pizza combined, and it happened again.

"Please take a seat, young lady," the manager said. "I will call your Chase Bank in New York City."

Why did he have to call them? Could he just open the jaws of the ATM again and yank out my card?

People rushed in and out of his office. The telephone rang out of control. Buzzers went off repeatedly. It was like I was in a Fellini movie.

At 5:30 p.m., the bank was closing for a long holiday weekend, and I still did not have my card. Just as important as finding work in my strange new land was learning to adapt to its ways, bureaucracies, and hiccups.

I had only a few things at my disposal for calming down: naps, biscotti, cigarettes, wine, the gym, and a new man. I took the last two options.

I ran to the gym in form-fitting sweatpants and had barely done a few crunches before a handsome Italian guy came over and introduced himself. I had seen him around the gym before—a clean-looking guy named Gianni who turned out to be an architect who also spoke English. Maybe this one didn't carry a gun. Maybe this one would know how to kiss. Maybe this one would be beautiful, like the Tyrolean Sea, but not polluted like it as well.

Gianni was *in punto*, on time, to take me to dinner at a cute restaurant on the Tiber. I managed to speak Italian with him for two hours, until the stroke of 11:00 p.m. when my bilingual spigot always seemed to turn off. "Beh … I'm done with Italian for the night," I said.

Gianni was a gentleman. He kissed me goodnight on both cheeks and offered to help me move into my new apartment. I was beginning to love Rome again.

On moving day, my Peruvian friend Manuel helped me take my five large Tumi suitcases to the bat cave across the river. There, my feet would not turn black from the dirt, although I wouldn't be able to walk barefoot there for a different reason: the stone floor was as cold as a freezer. I needed to buy *pantofole*, slippers.

Gianni, my new possible *ragazzo*, boyfriend, also showed up to help, but when we arrived at the new apartment, there was no hot water.

Was it me and my poor luck? Or was Rome the city of no air conditioning and no hot water?

Gianni called the owner for me.

As an architect, he was handy in other ways as well. He pulled the gas stove out from the wall and examined the tubing for the gas line. "It's *rotto*, broken," he said. "It could explode."

When he went out and bought me a new tube and installed it for me, I knew I could fall in love with him. I dare any woman who is alone in a new country, who feels insecure and has childhood issues, to say otherwise.

"Alison, do you want to go out with me as my girlfriend?" he asked.

We were seated in my cold, dark new living room, on one of the many uncomfortable, unforgiving chairs. I merely nodded my head in assent.

That night, I looked forward to a long, hot bath. I let the tepid water run for a full hour before the first drizzle of warm water finally emerged from the faucet.

16

It was finally time to go observe the dubbing process at Associated Recording Artists. Instead of walking, I took the bus, but in the end, it would have been far easier to just walk there.

Frank, the dubbing boss who knew my acting teacher, greeted me warmly. He smelled of cigarettes and had a persistent, hacking cough, which seemed at odds with his profession of overseeing careful voice work.

The actors sat in a darkened studio with only a task light by which to read the script as they dubbed into English various films from Italy, Spain, and even Arabic countries. They were all professional dubbing actors, and some of them had been living in Rome for decades doing this highly skilled craft. Carol had told me that the pay was quite good.

I sat there for hours watching the dubbing actors at work. They had to say lines in English that did not match what the actors onscreen were saying in other languages, but by studying mouth movements and by other tricks of the trade, they were able to dub almost seamlessly. It was fascinating to watch and looked quite difficult, but I hoped that one day this was where I would report to work—to a darkened room with a task light, and to Frank as my new boss.

I emerged from the darkness into a brilliant Roman sun, which felt good after my dark, cold apartment. In the summer they don't have enough air conditioning, and in the winter they don't turn on the heat until Nov. 15.

By now I had been back to New York to visit the Italian consulate for my paperwork and could return to the local *questura*, police station, to hand in my forms for the *permesso di soggiorno* that would allow me to stay longer in Italy as a worker, not a tourist. I had already lived in Rome for six months, well over the limit. Without this *permesso*, I wouldn't be able to get the work *permesso*, and then I wouldn't be able to work at all.

I brought with me bank statements, a copy of my passport, plus four passport photos. The concierge at the Residence, with whom I had remained friendly, had helped me find a notary public, a man with lots of gold jewelry who charged way more than was probably legal to apply a stamp to a piece of paper.

Nothing is simple in Italy. Naturally, when I got to the *questura*, a *polizia* told me to come back after their lunch break. I returned right on the dot of 1:00 p.m., even walking through the dark tunnels of Rome that frightened me, and there wasn't a soul inside.

Finally, at 1:30 they began staggering in and re-opened the station. I was the first in line.

"You need a letter from the owner of your apartment," the policeman said in Italian.

"I have a copy of my rent check," I told him.

"We also need a letter from her that confirms you are paying rent."

I hadn't really warmed to Camilla or she to me, and the thought of asking her for a favor didn't thrill me. I had a feeling she wasn't paying taxes on the extra apartment income and didn't want to declare it to the government.

She did not return my calls until four days later.

"I must get this letter so I can stay in Italy," I explained in Italian.

"I don't know," she said. "I am treating you like a guest in my apartment, not a tenant."

"But I'm paying you rent. Guests don't pay rent. Please, I really need this letter."

She reluctantly agreed to write the letter, but could not guarantee when it would be done. I called her "boy helper," Carlo, every day to see if he was coming with the letter. I was about to give up hope when Carlo showed up a week later with the letter.

Once again at the police station after their break. Once again, they were nowhere in sight at the appointed time, and I had to wait.

"*Signora* Rand." They were calling my name the more formal way.

Finally, I had my *permesso di sorgiorno*. I was now legally and officially allowed to remain in Italy for an entire year.

It was quite an accomplishment. Lesser people would have given up by now. Of course, I still needed to get a work permit—and some work—but if I had come this far, I believed I could go the distance.

Going the distance, as it turned out, involved losing a few jobs first. The one that really hurt was my role in *The Eighteenth Angel*, an Italian movie about a modeling agency that signs pretty young women just to collect souls for Satan. I was all ready to sell my soul to get this role, hopefully as one of the model sacrifices. I had even signed a contract and been fitted for my costume before they called to tell me I was off the picture because I didn't have my *permesso di lavoro*. "But the casting agent told me I didn't need it for this one time!" I protested.

"Sorry, ees not possible."

I tried everything I could. I wrote to the Italian consulate and sent letters from others on my behalf. I applied in whatever order they told me, although it always seemed as if they made up new rules every time I asked. I jumped through all the hoops and hoped that by working as a dubbing actress for a corporation, with Frank as my boss, I would eventually get my permesso di lavoro.

By now I was seeing more of Gianni. He had even given me my own helmet to wear for when he took me out on his scooter—for my safety, as well as perhaps for stopping me from digging my nails into him when I hung on for dear life. I thought it was the sweetest thing any man had done for me in Italy, or maybe even in the United States.

We cooked pasta in my kitchen to celebrate our new relationship. He spent the night, but we didn't have sex; I liked that we were taking this relationship slow. He held me in his arms, and it felt nice to just lie in bed all night with a man. *Grazie Dio per i tappi*, thank God for earplugs. He snored like an airport runway.

I finally had my first audition for a dubbing job, for a low-budget German movie being dubbed into English. I knew I had only ten minutes of hot water to try and wash my long, thick hair before it was *finito* for the hot water. Despite Gianni's help with the stove, I still had problems, which were confirmed when two *idraulici*, plumbers, with identically unshaven faces, poked around my kitchen with flashlights and checked the wiring throughout the apartment and pronounced: *tutto è rotto*. Everything is broken. They said they'd be back.

The good news is that I landed the dubbing job.

At last, my first real work in Italy! It came just in time since my bills were adding up and I had forfeited two months' rent in giving up my first apartment.

I was now officially a dubbing actress. At first, I was nervous, which made my throat dry as if I had eaten peanut butter. But gradually I relaxed and was able to follow the German actress' lips on the gigantic screen. When she said, "*Ich bin auf der suche nach einem arzt*," I said, "I am looking for the doctor," maneuvering my mouth into all kinds of contorted positions so that it took just as long for me to say it in English as for her to say it in German.

When the director called, "That's a day," I knew I had succeeded.

The audition was fine, but I was happy to get away for the weekend with Gianni to his parents' weekend home in Ansedonia. His parents wouldn't be there, so we would have the place to ourselves. Perhaps it was time to achieve a new level of intimacy in this relationship.

It was a two-hour drive. Once we were out of Rome, the air was cleaner. The house had a direct view of the indigo-blue Tyrolean Sea. It was shaping up to be a fine getaway … except that the two-story house was not very clean. I jumped when a spider crawled up my leg and tried to contain my angst when I saw ants crawling near me on the floor. "Take off your shoes and relax," Gianni said. I kicked off my shoes, despite the ants, and felt particles of sand beneath my toes from the living-room rug.

Except perhaps for the spiders and the ants and the sand, it was still looking like a promising weekend. We shopped at a local food store and together cooked pasta and prawns in his parents' large, rustic kitchen. After dinner, we made love for the first time.

It was very quick.

It's not that I demanded perfection, but a few compliments or kind words would have been nice. I chalked it up to how sometimes the first time in bed is not so great because two people have to get to know each other better. The rest of the weekend would be better.

The next day, Gianni stayed out for hours playing tennis with a friend while I stayed home alone with the ants and the spiders. When he returned, we again cooked dinner in the rustic kitchen and again made love.

This time was worse than before. Was he trying to beat his own speed record? If so, he succeeded.

He must have known I was disappointed. "*Penso di avere un problema con l'intimità*," he said, admitting that he might have a problem with intimacy.

"I like you a lot," I offered. "Maybe this just needs a little fine-tuning."

I knew our sex life would need more than that. I knew he showered, yet he had a distinctive odor in a distinctive place. I kept wondering what in the world could possibly create that, but I was not going to cause him anxiety and further speed up his timing by asking him.

In the morning, we rode bicycles along a forest path near the beach. It brought me an inner peace I had not previously experienced in Rome. Perhaps this was the tradeoff I would have to make—pleasant company with a nice man, in exchange for very bad sex.

When I got home, my psychiatrist landlady finally sent over a woman to clean my apartment, something that should have been done before I moved in.

Stefania, the cleaning lady, arrived with an entire suitcase of equipment. The first—and only—thing she did was to blow out the washing machine. The moment she pressed the ON button, there was a strange squeak and then a loud pop, and then complete darkness. All the lights had blown.

Stefania became a detective, using my flashlight to check the wiring and the fuse box, just as the plumbers had done, except that Stefania was able not only to diagnose the problem but also to find what was apparently the only solution to my apartment woes:

"*Non è possible utilizzare la lavatrice e accendere le luci contemporaneamente*." It was not possible to use the washing machine and have any lights on at the same time.

17

Maybe nothing in my apartment worked, but I was a real dubbing actress now. Buoyed by my success, I changed my outgoing answering-machine message to one in Italian:

Questa è la segreteria di Alison. Per favore, lasciate un messaggio dopo il beep.

Italians always said I sounded very American—which they thought was *affacinante*, charming, but I'd been practicing and practicing to try to sound more Italian.

I called my brother and asked him to call me back and leave me my first message. I let it play without picking up so he could hear my Italian.

"Hey, little one," he said into the machine, and then cleared his throat. "Is that you? Or an Italian lady living in your house?"

I called him back, thrilled, but I was concerned about his voice. It didn't sound strong.

"Well, It's not a great day," he confessed—which was a lot, considering that he never complained about himself.

I was always worried about David's health. His Crohn's disease, a severe autoimmune illness, had gotten worse over the years. Our father had died relatively young, at 57, of a heart attack, and David was really the only solid male figure in my life who had ever looked out for me. He sent me special letters on my birthday: "I am the most fortunate brother in the world to have you as my sister." He always made himself available to talk to me, no matter when or how often I called, and had been rock-solid in his support of me over the years. He listened tirelessly to my boyfriend woes and soothed me whenever I called him crying. It thoroughly shook me to hear him sounding weak.

"Don't worry, it will pass," he assured me.

I was trying to take things one day at a time in my new life in Rome and live for the moment, but it was always a struggle. I was a planner by nature, but in Rome, it was the art of *ci sentiamo dopo*. Literally, it means I'll catch you later, but in Rome "later" could be any time later that day, week, or month.

Or more. As with Alberto, who called me out of the blue, months after he said he would make a "decision" as to whether he wanted to make me his girlfriend.

During our conversation, I asked him if he wanted to have dinner, and he answered, "*Com'è no*," why not. I had hoped for something a little more muscular, a little more enthusiastic. "That's okay, I've changed my mind," I said, lighting a cigarette and feeling more confident. "Maybe dinner another time."

I was still seeing Gianni, but he was always in Ansedonia with his parents and sisters on weekends. Finally, he invited me there to meet his family—or maybe he just happened to invite me for a weekend when his family just happened to be there. It was hard to tell if there was a deeper significance to the invitation.

Gianni picked me up from the train at Ansedonia with a smile and a hug.

Gianni introduced me to his parents with, "This is my friend, Alison," in Italian, and immediately retreated to another room, leaving me alone with them. There was also one of his sisters, Rita, whose 2-year-old was having a screaming fit.

Apparently, no one was expecting me, and Gianni hadn't told them anything about me. The parents looked up from where they were reading on the couch and said ciao before going back to their books.

For the first two hours of that weekend, I felt as if I were inside a thick, dense forest of stress. The rest of the weekend was not much better. I smiled like an idiot, my heart beating rapidly. My Italian had significantly improved, but it slipped the minute I became anxious.

When Gianni returned after what felt like an entire day had passed, we went into his room, and I began to cry.

"I'm not going to sleep with you here," I said.

"That is best," he agreed.

"Why did you invite me at all?"

"I don't know," he confessed. "I think I am afraid of women."

"Great," I muttered.

We got through the evening by going to a movie and then out to dinner with some of his friends. Sad and lonely, I went to sleep in a separate room.

In the morning, I had a change of spirit. I told myself that I must learn to accept the discomfort of the moment and try to be happy. Activity would be good. I had brought along my Italian homework, so I began studying more complicated tenses and learning new vocabulary while sitting in the kitchen.

"*Buon giorno, ragazzi*," good morning kids, Gianni's mother said as she opened the kitchen shutters all the way. "*Che giorno bellissimo.*" What a beautiful day.

"*Il café è eccelente.*" All I could think to say was that the coffee was great. I added that she had a great son.

"Oh, but he is 43 years old and alone," she replied in Italian. I might have been able to shed some light on that for her, but I simply smiled.

Gianni was distant the rest of the weekend, even when we were riding bikes together.

"I don't want to be anyone's boyfriend," he finally told me. "Listen, if I don't fall in love in a month, then I'm not involved."

"Huh?" I said. "Where did *that* come from?"

He shrugged.

"You know, life doesn't work like a clock," I said. "Maybe you need to give this more time."

"I like you *molto*, very much, but I'm not involved," he said.

When I got back to my cold, lonely apartment, I counted out my six biscotti and made myself a cup of tea.

The following morning, I woke up sick with what felt like another virus, like the kind I'd had over the summer. My legs and muscles ached, and my skin felt rubbed raw. My stomach was queasy, and I had no energy. I skipped the gym and my Italian lessons and my acting class.

I was grateful when Carol, my acting teacher, called to check up on why I'd missed class.

"I'm feeling crummy," I said. "Physically and romantically."

I told her about Gianni. "You can't change him, so concentrate on changing yourself and your behavior," she advised. She sounded wise, but I wasn't sure exactly what was wrong with my behavior. I was kind and polite and tried to act loving and encouraging with boyfriends. Was that a bad thing? It was as if my neediness were lit up on a giant billboard for all to see and laugh at.

"Do you have a doctor?" Carol asked me.

"I saw Dr. Stessi over the summer for bronchitis," I said.

"That star fucker, forget him," she said. "I'll give you someone better."

She gave me the name of an American doctor. This one, Dr. Levi, wasn't sure what was wrong with me but thought it was a "virulent virus" and sent me for blood tests. Naturally, there was another *schopero*, strike, that day, which meant it would be an *incubo*, nightmare, to get to the lab. Nevertheless, I managed to get a bus before the strike began, and had four vials of blood drawn. By the time I was finished, the strike was on, and I had to walk most of the way home in my weakened condition before I was able to find a taxi.

Luckily, despite all my boyfriend problems, there was a young man who was able to give me some needed attention while I was sick. It was Federico, the hairdresser who'd been cutting my hair for a while—and by "young man," I mean he was about 12 years younger than me. The first time I met him, he delicately washed my thick hair in the sink and then as he was combing out the tangles I spotted the familiar sight of infatuated eyes staring limpidly down at me.

"You are very beautiful," he told me in Italian. "Will you have dinner with me?"

"Thank you," I told him, "but I think I am much older than you."

This did not seem to dampen his ardor as he massaged conditioner onto my ends.

He kept asking me to dinner, and I finally settled on lunch. Federico had a sweet, suave way about him as he pulled the chair out for me, or stood when I got up to visit the ladies' room and again when I returned. His aftershave was not too sweet, and I enjoyed his company. He took me to see *The Bridges of Madison County* in English, where I ran into my Italian teacher in the theater. "He is very cute, *cara*," Flavia whispered to me. "He seems comfortable with himself."

Federico even took my hand in the movie theater, something Gianni had never done. He had twinkling brown eyes and turned out to be a great kisser.

Although things never progressed very far with him—I hadn't allowed it yet—Federico called constantly once he knew I wasn't feeling well. He brought me groceries and never asked for payment. He made me soup. He also insisted on kissing me, which was rather unpleasant while I wasn't feeling well, but otherwise, his behavior was very sweet.

He brought me water. He brought me toilet paper. "*Ti voglio bene*," he said.

I love you.

It would have been one of the most romantic moments in my life, except that I was sick, and except that he followed that up pretty soon with, "*Voglio fare l'amore con te*," I want to go to bed with you. Which was not quite as romantic as his first declaration of love.

Although Gianni checked in with me from time to time, he was dismissive of my illness, insisting that it was nothing. The women I knew in Italy expressed their friendship but never seemed to have time for me.

After eight days of feeling progressively worse, I decided after checking in with my mother that I should go home and visit her for the holidays.

Even Flavia, the Italian teacher who had said I was like a daughter to her, had been acting differently toward me lately. When she heard I was going back to the States for the holidays, she brought a giant box wrapped in paper and asked that I take it with me in my luggage to give to her boyfriend back home.

"It's rather large," I said. "I'm not sure I'll have room for that."

She wouldn't tell me what was in the box and seemed miffed that I wouldn't take it for her. "Can't you mail it from here?" I asked her.

After that, she suddenly stopped calling me "*cara,*"dear, and started canceling our lessons, too.

Spending a few weeks back home was good for me. I saw my friend Denise in New York, let my mother and George pamper me in Florida, and saw American doctors in both cities who brought me back to health. My mom and I spent quality time staying up late, talking and knitting. "I'm proud of you, honey," she told me. "I could never do what you've done." I had always lived to please her, and it was a rush to feel that I had succeeded.

When I returned to Rome in January 1996, my young Italian hairdresser was waiting at the airport to greet me. He had called me at my mother's place on Christmas Day, a lovely surprise.

We kissed at the arrivals gate like new lovers, eager to hold each other again. Somehow, he managed to get my huge black suitcases into his tiny, efficient Renault.

While driving back to my apartment, he turned silent. "*Dimme tutto*," I said. Tell me everything.

"I am afraid," he said. "I don't want to fall in love with you."

"What's changed?" I asked, but he wouldn't answer.

I was frustrated, and nearing the end of my patience. What was it with these Italian men? What didn't I understand about them, or about me?

We arrived at my apartment to find that there was no hot water. Too jet-lagged to care, I lay on the bed with Federico, and within a moment there was a giant cracking sound. The mattress fell through the broken frame to the floor. Under other circumstances I might have laughed, but not now.

"I am afraid you will not stay in Italy," Federico said. "I don't want to get hurt."

"What do you mean? I really like it here," I said from a mattress on the floor of an apartment with no hot water.

18

I couldn't have been happier to tell the taxi driver where I wanted to go. "Cinecittà, *per favore*."

I had won the part in the Stallone movie.

It was a small part, to be sure, but from the pride I felt, the sense of accomplishment, the pure joy radiating from every pore, you'd think I had won the lead.

The casting director Shaila Rubin, who said that for this one time I would not need a work permit, had called me in for a wardrobe fitting—not in a costume to sell mozzarella cheese or dry crackers, but to be a part of a major American action film to be shot here at Italy's most famous movie studio. The greats had walked here, in costumes involving gladiatorial lace-up sandals and Western gunslinger-wear. I would walk here, too, in a form-fitted beige-and-blue uniform to play an employee of the control center of the Port Authority of New York and New Jersey. It sounded very grand, although it was a very small part, but any part at this point in my career was a big part. I planned to be the best control-center worker in the filmic history of the Port Authority. When I announced that people were victims of a fireball inside the Holland Tunnel, I would be the most distraught, the most anxious.

I did anxiety well.

Cinecittà was on the outskirts of Rome. I figured that with my tunnel-phobia it was easier to take a taxi to my fitting than to walk underground in search of the Metro.

The fitting itself hardly took a few minutes. The filming would take place over one or two days in late January.

Waiting for the call that announced my actual shoot date was sheer agony. When would they call? When would they call? I told my mother I hated Italy and wanted to go home; this country was both *paradiso* and *inferno,* and I often couldn't tell which was which. But the call finally came on a Monday to be there the next morning at 10:00 a.m.

I took another taxi for 50,000 *lire,* about $30. When I arrived, there were at least fifty other extras milling about, along with the many crewmembers you'd expect on a large-budget American action film.

Just as in New York, being an extra on a film mostly requires sitting around and waiting. That is also true for the stars, since there is a lot of down-time on a film set while camera crews set up and set decorators decorate, and everyone checks their sound levels and equipment, and producers deal with crises, weather, and whatnot. The only thing that was different was that catering gave us paninis for lunch instead of hot dogs.

"Do you think we'll get to meet Stallone?" I asked another extra, a German man named Dirk who was also supposed to be a control-center staffer in the movie.

"I haven't seen him," said Dirk in Italian. "I don't think he has any scenes today."

I was disappointed, but maybe I'd see the star on the red carpet at the movie's premiere! Not that I thought all the extras would be invited to that, but a girl can dream.

The set I'd be working on was for the busy control room, but the major set they had erected at Cinecittà for this movie was a big, fake entrance to the Holland tunnel. It looked more or less like the real thing, with paved lane lines and steel barricades, but was far cheaper to construct here than in New

York or Los Angeles. There was no way they could shut down the real thing so they could film explosions while hundreds of thousands of motorists waited to get through the tunnel to their jobs and appointments on the other side.

As I walked onto the control-room set, I mentally rehearsed the lines they had given me at my audition, imagining different ways I could deliver those lines. "There's a toxic fire! The fire is TOXIC! Oh my God, a toxic fire is RAGING ... I'm on it, Captain." But it turned out that they didn't expect us in the control tower to say any line in particular, just react to the imagined horror of the Holland Tunnel being blown sky-high.

In all, they filmed us for seven hours reacting to the explosion and looking alarmed and panicked. Although I often felt alarmed and panicked while living in Rome, for seven hours I felt sheer enjoyment—it was fun to be on a real movie set, making real money.

Dirk, the German I'd met on the catering line, offered me a lift home on the back of his navy-blue BMW motorbike. I held tight to his waist as we zigged and zagged through the traffic. We were back to the center of the city in 20 minutes.

"Do you want to have dinner with me?" he asked, and we found a cute spot in Trastevere, the Greenwich Village of Rome, where my acting teacher lived. We had linguine *con fungi porcini*, and grilled fish.

"I'll help you get more work with Shaila," he offered. "I know her well."

"I'd be grateful," I said with a flirtatious smile.

It had been a perfect day. After we finished our dinner, he reached across the table and kissed me. Then he suggested we "go a Romano," split the check.

"I'll call you," he said before riding away on his BMW bike. I knew he wouldn't, and I was glad.

In my dark, cold apartment, nothing worked. My psychiatrist landlady always promised that a plumber would come *domani*, tomorrow. It was always *domani*.

The two plumbers finally showed up, Camilla told me I would have to pay for a new *scaldo bagno*, hot water heater. Even after it was installed, it didn't work properly. I had the two-minute shower down to a science, and nothing improved. All the plumbers did, as far as I could tell, was leave dirt tracked in from their boots, and ashes from their cigarettes.

Finally, Camilla sent her houseboy, Carlo. He brought me a new refrigerator that didn't leak, and he fixed my broken box spring on the bed.

Then the new refrigerator began to leak too. An electrician arrived and told me I was lucky to be alive with all the dangerous fuses in my apartment.

I moved back to the Residence.

I didn't tell Camilla I was leaving; I simply left. I felt I didn't owe her another month's rent if she didn't care that I was living in an unsafe space.

Telling her would have been easier. Instead, I felt I had to avoid her, and she lived only a five-minute walk from the Residence. Every day I wore dark sunglasses and a hat and poked my head around corners to check if the coast was clear before proceeding. I probably looked like a criminal.

The new room at the Residence was tiny, but it was clean and nice. I relaxed enough to call a new guy, someone who had been suggested to me by a friend I'd made from one of my dubbing jobs. "Renato is intelligent, successful, and very handsome," she said.

"Is he nice?" I asked.

"He's great."

I met Renato for dinner at a small, quaint restaurant near the Residence. He was short but had a cute, boyish look, with dark brown hair and an engaging smile. He dressed like a preppy American in a Ralph Lauren shirt and sweater. He spoke English well, but I wanted to practice my Italian, so we made a deal, *lo scambio*: one hour in one language, the next in the other.

Renato turned out to be a good kisser. He was also an expert at quickly unhooking a bra with one hand, but I stopped him.

"I need to go slowly," I said.

"*Va bene, amore*," he said. All right, love.

We dined together. We attended a Caravaggio exhibit together. And it was Renato to whom I turned when Camilla's lawyer sent me a letter threatening to sue me for that final month's rent.

Renato was consoling. Through his questions, I was able to remember that the woman I had met on the plane when I was moving here had given me several contacts, including my Italian teacher, and including a lawyer.

I found the card with the lawyer's name and met with her—if by "met with her" I mean an hour of me crying and sobbing while trying to explain the house of horrors that had been Camilla's apartment: the dangerous wiring, the leaky refrigerator, the lack of hot water, the broken furniture...

"Don't worry. Please don't worry," she said.

I met with her on a Saturday, and by the close of business on Monday the legal matter was dropped and forgotten. The lawyer wouldn't even let me pay her.

Meanwhile, Renato helped me find a new apartment—my third so far in Rome. My fifth, if you count my two stays at the Residence.

My new place was a large, bright studio on a charmingly sloped street near my familiar Piazza del Popolo. I even loved the name of the street, Via Principessa Clotilde. It sounded like a royal address.

It was an upscale building with views of Villa Borghese. The studio was small, with a sliding door to wall off the sleeping area, and a kitchen even smaller than the munchkin one I had in the Residence, but the bathroom was large and had a gigantic, sunken tub, along with the hot water that would go in it.

It was perfect.

What wasn't perfect was my new relationship with Renato. It took a nosedive the minute I moved into my new place.

"I don't want to continue with you after we sleep together ten times," he announced to me one afternoon.

"*Come?*" What?

"I like you, but after the tenth time, I will stop us because I will get too attached and then you will return to New York and then what for me? That is not good."

Ten times and I was out, just like that.

The good news about my new apartment was that it had hot water and also lots of light. The bad news was that the light came from the windows, but not from anything plugged into an electrical outlet. One day, I couldn't turn anything on, from the TV to the bedside lamp.

The owner of the apartment, Clara, said she would send the electrician. I wasn't crazy about this electrician, since he had been here for a previous check, and his smile had lingered too long, but I needed to be able to turn on a switch.

The overly friendly electrician returned. I asked him how much I had to pay him for this visit.

"*Preferisco un bacio a pagamento,*" he said. He preferred to be paid with a kiss and tried to collect on the debt right away by pressing his long body against mine.

I backed away.

"No," I said, startled. "*Preferisco pagarla.*" I preferred to pay him in cash.

He opened his arms wide as if he expected me to jump into them.

"*Basta,*" I said. Enough. "*Ecco i soldi e buon giorno.*" Here is your money and good day.

He left without complaint. I had just figured out how the Roman women handled things.

Living in Italy was amounting to endurance training. But one thing I was learning was that being overly friendly was considered polite back home and something else entirely here.

19

I was becoming a little more Roman all the time. I now allowed myself five cigarettes a day, up from two. I justified it because so many people there smoked and I wanted to fit in.

I was eating more, too. My six biscotti every night were starting to show up on my thighs. I ate them whenever I felt anxious, and I felt anxious a lot. Even the sweet Italian masseuse, Lia, noticed. "Your legs are retaining water," she told me.

I continued to re-evaluate my life in Rome every minute. Should I stay? Should I go? My emotions swung up and down. I had more dubbing jobs, and I had no end of "new boyfriends," but the boyfriends didn't last, and I wasn't sure what kind of life I was working toward here. Frank told me that if I wanted to continue trying to get the *permesso di lavoro*, I needed to become a resident first. I was on overload with all the requirements.

I dated Alessandro, a good-looking Italian guy from the gym -actually, all Italian men are good-looking. He seemed fine until he made an anti-Semitic remark about Jewish restaurant owners being cheap. "The Jews only want money," he said.

I met another guy at the gym, Fabio, who did not speak much English. He didn't have all that much to say in Italian, either.

"*Come sta tuo lavoro?*" How was work? I asked him over a fish dinner.

"*Bene.*"

After our meal, he magically began to show more interest in me, taking my hand and kissing me on the walk back to my apartment. "Can I come upstairs to kiss you goodnight?" he asked in Italian.

"No, it's better we say goodnight here," I said.

I had moved across the ocean, but in many ways, my life was falling into the same patterns as in New York: lots of anxiety, not enough work, and boyfriends who were interchangeable. My new landlady, Clara, said she could help with at least one of those areas.

"I know someone I can introduce you to," she said. "There's a lady who lives on the top floor. She is in the film world."

Clara wasn't kidding. The lady in the penthouse of my new building turned out to be none other than Lina Wertmüller—a famous Italian director, the first woman ever to be nominated for an Oscar for directing, and the *auteur* of such films as *Swept Away* and *Seven Beauties*.

"Really?" I said. "You know her?"

I was as nervous calling this upstairs neighbor of mine as I was before a first date. Lina's houseboy answered the phone, and then the *grande dame* herself was on the phone.

"Please stop up Sunday morning and we'll talk," she said graciously.

I couldn't sleep the night before. I tried sleeping on top of the sheets, under the sheets and twisted up in them. On Sunday morning I rampaged through my closets to find the right thing to wear.

I went upstairs and rang the bell at exactly 8:30 a.m. Vito, the houseboy, opened the door. He wore a smock over his clothing, as if he were a painter's assistant. "She is being interviewed for a magazine," he told me in Italian. "You can wait in the living room."

I was afraid to sit on the white couch, for fear that I would stain it with my perspiration, but all the fabric was in light colors. Lina herself was known for wearing white, right down to the frames of her eyeglasses.

Curious, I went over to the window, where I could see the director being interviewed out on the terrace. Lina, although nearly seventy at the time, was rocking a white bikini. She was on a lounge chair talking nonstop to a journalist.

This would take a while. I should have eaten something to absorb the acid sizzling away in my stomach, but every time Vito came in to ask if I wanted something, I felt faint with fear and decided to just do nothing; that not accepting a drink would somehow be safer, even though I was parched.

Finally, after nearly two hours, the interview ended and Vito took me out on the terrace to meet his boss.

"What a pleasure to meet you," I said with a grin that was too big and a handshake that was overly firm. My stomach made loud, strange sounds that I'm sure everyone in Rome could hear.

"Come sit down," said Lina. "Would you like some yogurt or coffee?"

My stomach growled just hearing those words, but I declined.

Lina had whitish-blonde hair cut short. Her pink lipstick looked even brighter against the dazzling white of her bikini. She asked me all about my acting experience in New York and how I liked living in Rome. Gradually, I relaxed.

"I might have a part for you in a film I am making with Harvey Keitel," she said.

I thought I would collapse onto the terrace floor, and that Vito would have to come pick me up and fan me with the hem of his smock.

The rest of my visit was a blur. I have no idea what we discussed or what foolish thing I said. All I know is that I had promised to pick up a few items Lina wanted the next time

I visited my mother in the States: melatonin, Moon Drops perfume, and Nivea hand lotion.

I did happen to return to the States soon for a visit. As soon as I was back in Rome, I called Lina's apartment and arranged to bring her items upstairs to her.

Again she was on her terrace in a white bikini and the eyeglasses with the trademark white frames. "Melatonin, perfume, and Nivea," I announced as I took each item out of the plastic bag I was carrying and set them before her.

"Thank you, *cara*," she said.

"Is there anything new on your movie with Harvey Keitel?" I asked. The words were out of my mouth before I realized how awful that sounded, as if I expected her to give me a role just because I had brought her some hand lotion and didn't ask for any other kind of payment, but I was nervous.

"I will be casting in April," she said.

"Please think of me for a part of any size," I said. Could I sound more craven?

"*Si, cara*. I will."

Some problems in Italy I was learning to handle. When the electric company overcharged me by the equivalent of hundreds of dollars, I called them and told them firmly in Italian that there was a problem with my bill.

"What is the problem, lady?" the woman asked in Italian.

"It's much too high," I said.

She put me on hold, checked her computer, and told me I was correct. Was that the end of it? That was just the start. I needed to wait two weeks for a letter from them. Then I had to send a fax along with previous bills. Nothing is easy in Italy, from crossing a street to paying a bill.

At least I was able to handle that one. The day my apartment was infested with a horde of gargantuan bees, I had to run for help to Vito, Lina Wertmüller's houseboy.

Vito rushed in with a fly swatter and a can of bug spray. Whenever he heard a BZZZZZING, he swatted and sprayed.

"Whenever you need me, just call," he left saying. "And don't open the windows."

My mother and stepfather paid me another visit. Together, we were going to drive to Tuscany for a week.

They picked me up in a rental car, and I showed off my new (third) apartment, and my improved grasp of the language. We stayed at a hotel in Chianciano Terme near Sienna, a place that was known for the curative powers of its water. Maybe the water could help wash away some of my persistent stress. Our hotel was a grand, old-world type filled with elegance and Italian sophistication.

During our dinners together, the three of us were seated in the inside ring of the large round dining room while all the single Italian men and women were seated around the circumference. The headwaiter explained that they came to the hotel in search of an *amante*, lover. "After dinner, they converge in the lobby to pick and choose with whom they will spend the night," he told us.

After the waiter left, George imitated him, elaborating on what the night would bring for these hopeful singles. We laughed, although my laughter was tinged with a bit of discomfort. How was my dating life all that different?

While my mother was there, I relaxed somewhat, but it concerned me that she wasn't feeling too well throughout the trip. She grimaced in pain every time she stood or sat down, chalking it up to a "stiff back." She was not much of a complainer. Once she was back in Florida, she discovered that she had a broken vertebra.

I hoped that maybe it was the curative power of the waters of Chianciano Terme that had as much to do with my calmed state as seeing my mother. Either way, my mother was gone, and I was back in Rome, so I went where I go when I need my "fix": the gym.

The gym was my all-purpose candy store: I got my dose of endorphins, and I also happened to spot a new guy asking about the bike room. He was well muscled, and when I heard him talking to the receptionist by the entrance, all I could think was: *he's American*!

He took the bike next to mine. It turned out that Martin was a geologist, originally from Chicago but now living in Saudi Arabia. It was his first time in Rome.

He asked me to dinner. I suggested Dal Bolognese, where I'd once eaten with Rocco so long ago. Inexplicably, many Roman restaurants had unkind lighting, but the soft lighting here, even without candles, gave everyone a glow.

That night, Martin and I were the first to be seated and the last to leave. We couldn't get enough of each other. His constant focus on me made me feel wanted and sexy. He talked about having a troubled past involving drugs and homelessness, but he seemed utterly stable now, from his sparkling appearance to how he talked about his work as a senior geologist. Over dinner, I allowed myself to be drawn in. It felt fun and reassuring. I invited him back to my place "for a few minutes," and we kissed for an hour.

The next night, dinner again—this time at a place on a sloping street. This time, however, the conversation didn't flow as freely.

"Tell me about living in Saudi Arabia," I said, trying to draw him out. "What do you do for fun there when you're not working?"

"Um, well, I watch videos and go to the gym."

"Do you have a lot of friends there?"

"A few."

The conversation wasn't sparkling, but we had surprising chemistry in bed. Unlike the Italian men, Martin liked to cuddle. I saw him every night, and most of the afternoons he was in Rome.

"Are you seeing anyone in Saudi Arabia?" I asked him while we were having dinner near the Pantheon.

"I see a few different women for company but no one special," he said.

I shouldn't have been prying. I wished I could tame my anxieties, be a person who didn't apply pressure by asking a man too many questions too early in a relationship, but I couldn't help myself. I was already pushing him away, and the more he pulled away, the more I pushed—to the point where he announced he wouldn't stay over with me on his last night in Rome, although it was okay to have dinner. "I feel I need to take a step back," he said in explanation.

We ate that last night at Mario dei Fiori and spent more time talking to the couple from Michigan at the next table than to each other. After dinner, we walked to the Trevi Fountain. Like any tourist, I threw a coin and made a wish: *Please, let something good work out for me in Rome.*

The next afternoon, Martin dropped by with a large bouquet of red roses, but it felt strained between us.

"Did I do something?" I asked, although I knew I had. I had been too needy. It was a sin in the dating world to appear to be needy, even if that was what I was.

"You are an A+," he said. "But it developed too quickly, and I can't give you what you need."

We made love one last time and then he was gone, back to Saudi Arabia and his occasional, not-special girlfriends, which is what I had been after all. Not special. I tried not to think about it, but I had a panic attack on the Stairmaster the next day. My body was doing the thinking for me.

20

It wasn't any one thing, but suddenly it seemed as if an avalanche of ailments had begun.

A few years before, I had suffered from a torn retina, which had me seeing floaters and dots in one eye as if there were bats flitting through the room, along with brief flashes of light. The eye doctor had told me it tore because I was nearsighted, and after mending it with laser surgery he warned me that one day it might happen to the other eye, too. Now, a few months after I had moved to my Via Principessa Clotilde apartment, I saw those spots and flares again, now in my right eye.

I asked Manuel at the gym if he knew of a retinologist. "You're in luck, lady," he told me. "Dr. Villi is here working out today. I'll call him over."

The doctor was reassuring. "Please, do not worry," he said. "Come to my clinic tomorrow, and I will take a look."

Dr. Villi was in his early forties, with dark, Roman features, including thick hair and a long-ish nose. I thought he was the most attractive man in the world at that moment just because he knew how to wield a laser, in case I needed eye surgery.

I arrived at Dottore Villi's office the next morning by taxi. It was a Catholic outpatient clinic that featured multiple statues of the Virgin Mary, as well as several paintings of Christ on the cross. I was ready to worship and believe, as long as the doctor could take away my problem and salve my worry.

His secretary, Anna, was especially nice to me. She held my hand as she put in the *gocce*, drops, to dilate my pupils. Forty-five excruciating minutes later, already imagining my impending funeral, Dottore Villi finally entered the room and peered into each eye. "It is all okay," he said.

"Okay?" I asked. "What does that mean? I see all kinds of shapes and lights!"

"Nothing new has torn, it is stable," he told me. "This happens to everyone at some point in their lives. Come back in a few weeks."

I would have married the good *dottore* right then and there, but the only thing he asked of me was to make a follow-up appointment with Anna.

"How much do I owe for today?" I asked Anna in Italian.

"Oh, you can pay next time," Anna said.

The next visit was the same—*gocce* in my eyes, a 45-minute wait, and Dr. Villi telling me that everything looked normal, that he would keep monitoring the situation.

"*Mi piacerebbe offrirti da bere o qualcosa, se vuoi o puoi*," I said, offering to take him out for a drink or something to thank him for his kindness.

"*Volentieri*," he said. With pleasure.

My heart beat like I had a crush on the boy in homeroom.

On the week that Dr. Villi had said was good for him, I came down with another virus or something. More flu-like symptoms, including my skin feeling so sensitive I didn't even want a sheet over it at night. Now I was anxious about having eye problems, health issues, and a drink with a handsome doctor that might, in fact, turn out to be a date. It wasn't an auspicious time to go through with this maybe-date, but I called his office anyway to firm up the time.

"He is doing laser surgery," Anna told me.

"I have a dubbing job and won't be home until 8:00 p.m.," I said.

"I'll give him your number, and he will call when he is free."

When I took a break during the dubbing job, I called again just to make sure the doctor and I were still on. Anna's voice was slightly less patient. "He is still in surgery, and he has your number," she told me succinctly.

When I got home, I dressed for the drink and waited. And waited. By 10:00 p.m., I knew the doctor was not going to call, and I went to bed.

I was really feeling like a loser. My emotional vulnerability was so great that apparently there was a giant neon sign on my head, flashing "NEEDY! NEEDY!" to any single, attractive male within three countries. Old eye problems were back, and the sinus problem I had developed in Rome resurfaced again as well. It didn't help that I had to breathe in the exhaust of a gazillion motorini and cars in the traffic-clogged center of Rome.

Since the female American doctor had not helped me last time, I paid a return visit to the self-proclaimed Doctor to the Stars, who gave me another antibiotic to try and told me he was going to call the "two best agents in Rome" on my behalf.

By the time I got back home, the Doctor to the Stars had already left a message on my machine to call Stefano, a top agent. The news did not excite me. I was tired of people bullshitting me all the time about things like agents who would boost my career and men who would boost my morale. The antibiotics weren't helping, either. There was something terribly wrong with my breathing, and I felt so dizzy at times that I could barely breathe at all.

"Keep all your windows closed at night," the Doctor to the Stars had told me, but when it was too warm and stuffy, I really had to open them. My third apartment didn't have air conditioning. I had spent over a million *lire* ($650) on doctors, and I still felt crummy. I lay in bed, listless and lightheaded, wondering again whether I should give up on my Roman adventure, and why I had ever thought it was a good idea in the first place.

The neon sign blinking on my head was warning off more than just the men. When I called Carol, my acting teacher, suddenly she was acting weird with me too.

"What's wrong?" I asked. "Did I do something to upset you?"

"I have to go," she said and hung up.

Huh? I had no idea what had happened. We hadn't had a disagreement. I always faithfully attended her classes, but now even that was no longer available to me. Her classes and the gym were the only two constants in my Roman world, and now I was down to one.

I had become friendly with Janie, a gorgeous British actress who helped out the casting agent Shaila Ruben sometimes. She came over and tried to comfort me.

I also called Derek, a friend I'd made on one of my dubbing jobs. Derek, from New Jersey, was tall and skinny and had long, shoulder-length, thinning hair. He was a film editor in Rome who did some dubbing on the side. He was married to an Italian woman and had two children, and we had both been hired for the day to "sigh" and "make love noises" for a soft-porn German film, so Derek was someone with whom I'd been intimate only aurally, in the recording studio.

"OOOOHHH. OOOOHHHHHH," I said.

"OHHHHH," Derek said in reply into the mic. "More. That's right!"

I felt the blood rush into my face from embarrassment every time I had to sigh. I was grateful it was dark inside the dubbing studio except for our task lights. In between takes, we'd both break into nervous laughter. From there, a friendship was born.

Now I told Derek that I was thinking of going back to New York. "I've been feeling sick for a long time, and there's not enough work to keep me here," I confided.

"Don't leave, honey," he said. "Listen, I'm going to introduce you to a friend of mine who's from the States. He's a film editor who just separated from his wife. What both of you need is good company."

"As long as he's normal," I said, only half-joking.

His friend Nelson turned out to be short and balding, but with an attractive face and smile.

"Hi, I'm Alison, Derek's friend," I said the first time we spoke.

"Hi, I'm Nelson. My wife just kicked me out." Those were his first words to me. That should have been a clue. There was something not quite right about Nelson.

"You know, I've got to get these hemorrhoids checked," he said one night after cooking dinner for me in my apartment. Not very romantic. And when I asked him to take his shoes off before making himself comfortable on the couch, he was a little too enthusiastic. "Oh, that feels good," he said. "Especially because I've got an ingrown toenail and it's killing me."

Nelson wasn't going to solve my problem. I was still lonely. It was an existential loneliness that wouldn't go away—like my virus, like the blockage in my nose. My fingers took control, as in a horror movie, dialing ex-boyfriends as if they had a mind of their own—Federico, the hair stylist. Gianni, the architect. Sometimes my calls went right to voicemail. Sometimes the guy picked up, and was cordial, or even expressed anew how he was here for me. But where was "here"? What did that really mean?

In the end, I was alone. I don't know if I'd have felt any differently had any of these men been by my side 24/7. Clearly, there was something fundamentally wrong with me. It was wrong to want, and I wanted. I lay in my bed in a kind of metaphysical fever, terrified for my future. Was it the fate of all humanity to remain alone? Or was it just me? Maybe everyone else was relatively happy and content, and it was just me who could not feel a sense of relief for more than a few minutes at a time.

I tried to give myself a reality check. I really had accomplished a lot in Rome, even with my initially shaky grasp of the language, and with knowing no one here and being saddled with stress and panic attacks and allergies and viruses. I had embarked on a steady new career as a dubbing actress and had already wrapped a role, however tiny, in a Sylvester Stallone action movie. I probably had more friends in Rome than I ever had at any one time in New York, thanks to all the dinners and parties I'd attended. But it was clear that I would have to go back to the States again for a little while, if only to see the doctors there and figure out what was wrong with me. I'd already been tested for mononucleosis and hepatitis, and I didn't have either of those.

I called my famous upstairs neighbor. "*Ciao*, Lina," I said. "I'm flying home to see my mom for a bit. Can I bring you anything?"

"Yes, *cara*," she said. "More Nivea."

21

I was just about to book my flight when I received a surprise call from a casting director about a film to be shown on the Rai Uno television channel owned by the media mogul and former prime minister Silvio Berlusconi. It was one of Italy's three big networks.

"We would like you to read for a part," they said.

This was big! I was torn, though. Now that I was determined to go back to the States for some rest, I almost didn't want to postpone it. But I did postpone it, just long enough that I could read for the part and see whether I got it. If I got it, obviously, I would have to stay in Rome, no matter what it took.

On the big day of my audition, I was brimming with confidence. "I like your look," the director said.

He told me to look at him, not directly into the camera, as he ran the lines with me. I was reading for a "best friend" type of role. It was a small part, but a good one, with multiple lines, even though I only did a few of them for the audition.

"Good reading," the director said when I finished. It sounded nice, but told me nothing.

Two weeks later, the director called to tell me they'd chosen someone else for the part of the best friend in the telefilm. I thanked him for letting me know. I'd become almost numb to disappointment. But before I left for the States in mid-December, I received a call with much better news.

"Congratulations," said Frank from the dubbing studio. "You are now an official member of Associated Recording Artists."

"You're kidding!" I squealed. "Really?"

In New York, I had never been able to get into SAG, the actors' union, but in Italy, I could now get contract work with A.R.A. It was quite an achievement.

Frank convinced me that becoming a resident was the only path to getting the *permesso di lavoro*. Before I went back to the States, Clara graciously offered to accompany me to fill out the residency papers.

We took a taxi and got to the office by 9:00 a.m., hoping to get in and out as quickly as possible. Instead, we stood in line for four hours, being pushed and shoved and having thick cigarette smoke blown in our faces. We were just nearing the front of the line when an official announced that they were closing for lunch.

Clara, who had been standing so patiently with me all this time, went ballistic. I didn't understand the Italian she spewed, but the guard must have understood quite well, because he sheepishly handed us the application so that we could fill it out.

Clara went down the list of requirements with me. "You need proof that you've lived here more than six months," she said.

"Check."

"You need proof that you have your own money from the States," she said.

"Check."

"And you need proof that you live alone, and not with a boyfriend."

"What?" I said. "You're kidding!"

The office of La Residenza would be sending an inspector to examine my apartment with forensic attention to detail to make sure I didn't have a boyfriend stashed away. This inspector would arrive within the next couple of months, between the hours of 7:00 a.m. and 7:00 p.m., with no advance notice.

"How will I know when he's coming?" I asked Clara.

"You won't."

On my flight to Miami, I met another Italian man, Matteo, on the plane. He was attractive and nicely dressed in a sports jacket and slacks. It was a pleasant 10 hours of conversation. "I'm visiting my son, who lives with my ex in Miami," he told me. His English was excellent, and we exchanged numbers.

My mother hooked me up with a doctor in Florida who confirmed that I had a virus, but didn't give me anything to help. "Just rest," he said.

"What about this rubbed-raw feeling on my legs?" I asked him.

"I can do some more blood tests, but it's probably the same virus. Just rest."

* * *

It was January 1997. In May I would have lived in Italy for two years.

Back in Rome, I returned to a machine full of messages, including one from Matteo, the man I had met on the plane. "*Chiamami al cellualre, per favore.*" Call me on my cell phone, please.

I called him back, but we played phone tag. He finally got me when he woke me after midnight.

"*Pronto? Qui è?*" I asked with a raspy voice.

"*Buona sera. Sono io. Matteo.*"

"It's really late."

"Let's make a plan to see each other," he said. He spoke with me for five minutes in English as quickly as if he were running from the law. I thought it was rude of him to call so late, but I told him I'd let him know when I felt better.

The next day I couldn't breathe and had a sore throat, but I went to the gym anyway, refusing to give in to this mysterious ailment.

I brought Lina her body cream. "*Grazie, cara,*" she said. I had set a bad precedent by never asking her to pay me back for these items, and it was too late to start now.

"Any news on your film?" I asked.

"Not yet, but soon. Maybe April or May."

A few days later I met Janie for a bite and gave her the pierced earrings I had bought for her in New York.

"Thanks," she said, "but my ears aren't pierced."

I guess I didn't know her as well as I'd thought.

Then she dropped a bombshell: She was moving back to London.

I didn't care why she was moving or what could have been troubling her in Rome. All I knew was that she had gradually become my closest friend here and that I was losing her. I felt as bereft as when a boyfriend broke up with me.

My lower lip began to quiver. "But…" I said.

"We can still talk by phone," she assured me.

"But I'm afraid to be here without you!" I said, starting to cry. "I need your support!"

I was only vaguely aware of how ridiculous this must have sounded. I didn't know Janie well enough to know what kind of earrings she preferred, yet suddenly my entire way of life seemed to depend on having her near me.

Okay, okay, I've got issues, I told myself. But just because I was aware of having issues didn't suddenly solve them for me. The thought of Janie leaving opened a chasm in my heart.

I took the only proactive step I could think of: I found an ear, nose and throat specialist who spoke some English.

"The smog here is a problem," he said as he positioned a tube down my nose and into my throat. "This is why your nose is blocked."

Finally, a reason. He prescribed a steroidal nose spray that seemed to help, at least a little.

"Smog and mold are the two things you need to fear," he said.

"But I live in the center of the city, which is smoggy," I said. "And I don't know whether my apartment has mold or not. What if it does?"

"Then you move to a new one," he said.

I called my architect ex, Gianni, to see if he knew of any mold-free apartments. "There's a unit available in the condo where I used to live," he told me. "I can show you if you're interested."

I was certainly more interested in the apartment than in Gianni at that point. I remembered visiting him in his old place and liking the area. It was only ten minutes from the city's center, only three tram stops from Piazza del Popolo, but the air was so much cleaner that it felt like another world.

Gianni took me to see it—an adorable one-bedroom with an extra room that had an uncomfortable blue love seat and a rickety old desk and chair. It had a big kitchen with a real freezer compartment in the refrigerator. Several of the windows faced the well-maintained condominium grounds, with a view of trees, bushes, and flowers. On the top floor was a large terrace space for hanging laundry. It felt perfect for me, and the air was considerably fresher.

Gianni said that the owner was a friend of his, another architect, but the best news was that this apartment was actually less money than what I was paying for my dusty, moldy, considerably smaller place. I liked Clara, my landlady, but I would blame my move on the smog, not on her apartment.

Fortunately, right before I moved, the inspector from the Residenza di Roma showed up to make sure I lived alone.

Had he shown up after I moved, he wouldn't have known where to find me, and I would have had to start that process all over again.

The inspector was an older man. He wore a raincoat and carried a small notebook.

"*Vive sola?*" he asked.

I assured him that yes, I lived alone. But my word was not enough, and he went around my tiny studio apartment, looking in the closet, under the bed, inside the bathroom, and even inside the tub, I guess in case I had a secret boyfriend secretly taking a bath. He scribbled many notes in his notebook.

I passed this rigorous test, and that's how I became an official resident of Rome.

I packed up my Italian life yet again, for my fifth move. Naturally, I asked Manuel at the gym to help me. He chuckled. "Of course I will help, lady." Manuel always came through for me.

Ten cartons, five large Tumi suitcases, and a boatload of angst. In addition to the two squirts of cortisone spray I was taking each day, I was taking Ativan at night to calm me down and help me sleep. I had come to Rome hoping it would give me a new life. But was Rome making me sick? Once again, I doubted the choices I'd made.

Right before my move, one of my agents sent me on another audition, this one for a commercial for an Easter candy. I had to do take after take while chewing a piece of chocolate and trying to look suggestive. The Italians were big on looking sexy while eating, and I wasn't very good at it. I popped the chocolate into my mouth and chewed it slowly as I puckered my lips. "YUMMM," I said.

"Again, please," the casting director said. "This time, don't squint your eyes."

"Oh, sorry," I said. "Was I squinting?"

"Again."

"YUMMMM," I said, forcing my eyes open as wide as they'd go. I probably looked demonic.

I called my agent to tell him I didn't think it went well. "Don't worry, *cara*," he said. "You look European, but maybe not as Italian as the other women. There will be another chance, I promise."

22

The fifth time was the charm.

I loved my new apartment. I woke up happy to see trees outside my window and smell air that wasn't clogged with motorini exhaust. My skin didn't have that fine layer of black soot it always collected within an hour of walking around in the center of the city. There was a noise problem at night—*ragazzi*, kids, hung out late between the buildings and talked and smoked, even on school nights—but my breathing was much improved. It seemed to come down to a choice between breathing and sleeping, and I had chosen breathing.

Matteo from the plane had been calling frequently. "Dinner at my house, tonight?" he asked, calling at the last minute.

"I'm busy," I said. "Maybe on another night with a little notice."

He called late. He called without notice. There was something insincere in his attitude that I didn't like. But my resolve to be treated with respect fell apart on a Sunday, my day of loneliness.

It was our first date, and my first time seeing where he lived. I wore a new pair of black fitted slacks with a low-cut blouse and worked on my hair for an hour trying to straighten out all the waves.

"Let's sit on the couch," he suggested when I arrived. I had to pick a few white tufts of cat fur off the fabric before

I sat. The TV was blasting the soccer match, and it was only halfway into the first half of the game.

As soon as his hands began to creep into my lap, I moved them away and asked where the bathroom was. While I was seated on the toilet, he opened the door without knocking.

I shrieked. "What are you doing?" I demanded.

"Oh, excuse me," he said, as if he had wandered into the wrong room in his own home by mistake.

When I was pulling my slacks back up, I saw in the full-length mirror that they were coated in white cat fur.

Although Matteo had invited me to dinner in his home, he hadn't cooked anything. He left it to his housekeeper. He must have neglected to tell her that I didn't eat meat because she tried to serve me bloody-rare beef, which I declined. She must have figured it out by the horrified look on my face because she came back from the kitchen a few minutes later with a salad and tuna fish.

After dinner, we returned to the couch. Now I could see what was leaving all that white fur around: a big, fluffy white cat was sitting dolefully on the armrest. I knew how she felt. I reached out to pet her, and she bit me. Twice.

That was just the beginning. There was the loud clacking sound that could only be dog toenails. They were coming my way, fast and clackety. A huge Doberman bounded into the room.

I adore dogs, but after my incident with the cat, I decided not to pet this member of Matteo's menagerie. In fact, no one was meant to pet this dog. He had a muzzle attached over his snout. With men, the warning signs weren't always clear to me, but this was a sign I knew how to read.

I couldn't envision the rest of the night watching soccer on TV and fending off Matteo's advances. I called a cab. Matteo was very nice to slip me the cab fare and make sure I called him to let him know I got home safely. "I've got business in

Germany next week," he said. "When I get back, let's go to Capri together."

Fed up with Italian men, I next dated a man I met at the gym from Switzerland.

Elias, a high-school science teacher, was quite attractive in a preppy kind of way, with dark brown hair and a small gold hoop in each ear. On the morning of our dinner date, I was bending down to pick up something from my kitchen floor when I jerked my back suddenly and *pow*. I could barely stand up. I had done this once before, many years ago, and it had been something to do with irritating the sciatic nerve, so I popped three Advil and hobbled over to a chair to rest. An hour later, I was able to move around, but I knew that I had hurt myself, and wondered how this would affect my date with Elias.

The Swiss are as known for being punctual as the Italians are not. Elias took it one step further—he was ten minutes early, and I wasn't ready yet. Because of the sciatica, I was also moving more slowly than usual.

Elias waited patiently outside my door. He looked gorgeous in a navy suit and red polka-dot tie. I wore a black wool dress, and I thought we made an elegant couple at the candlelit restaurant. We talked until closing time and then moved the conversation back to my place, on the uncomfortable blue love seat.

At around 3:00 a.m., he had a question for me. "May I kiss you?"

He was so charming; how could I say no?

We kissed for nearly two hours. I didn't let him stay over because the pain from my sciatica was worse, and now working its way down my left leg and up to my neck. But within a few days, Elias and I were in an actual relationship.

"I cannot stop thinking about you," he said. "This is very exciting. We have great chemistry."

I dove headfirst into being a couple—holding hands, gazing into each other's eyes.

It's not as if it was perfect. The same Swiss rigidity that made him hyper-punctual also made him find fault with the smallest things.

"Your second toe is a bit too long," he said one day when I was showing off my new pedicure.

"What? There's nothing wrong with my feet," I protested.

"Yes, look, it should be a little shorter than your big toe."

Still, he could be very sweet. "Hey, we should go to Capri for a weekend," he suggested. "Maybe sometime in May."

What was it about men and Capri? Did every man invite the new woman in his life to that island? Or was I just a Capri-magnet?

And then I made a mistake. One night, I stupidly allowed us to make love without a condom. From then on, I obsessed about whether I would get an SDT.

"I need you to take an AIDS test," I told him. I knew he was a cautious, clean person, but I still needed to see proof, so I could stop worrying.

"For your birthday present, I will do it."

"My birthday isn't for another few weeks."

"I am very busy with school right now. As soon as I get the chance, I will."

The weeks passed. I guess he didn't get the chance, because he never took the test. I took it myself, and it was negative, but I didn't trust Elias after that.

We broke up. We never did go to Capri.

My dependence on men bothered me. Capri was supposed to be one of the most beautiful places on earth. Why couldn't I just go by myself for a few days? I didn't need a man by my side to enjoy a refreshing few days by the beach.

I booked myself a nice hotel there for a long weekend. I took the train from Rome to Naples, and then the ferry to Capri. The ferryboat was overflowing with Japanese tourists taking pictures, and German tourists wearing socks with their sandals.

Once we docked in Capri, I was filled with pleasant antici-pation. I walked with my small-wheeled bag to the hotel, which looked pristine. My room was all white and had rose-colored marble floors in the bedroom and bathroom. There was a small balcony with a view of the Tyrrhenian Sea. I felt pampered in the king-sized bed and among the soft Italian linens and towels. Despite the sight of all the couples kissing and snug-gling with each other, I was determined to have a good time in Capri, all by myself.

I tossed and turned all night. It was stuffy and humid for mid-May, and there was no air-conditioning until June. The English-speaking CNN channel wasn't working. By morning, I was in no mood to meet the other guests in the dining room, so I ordered a continental breakfast from room service—*cor-netti*, the Italian version of croissants; freshly squeezed orange juice; and tasty, robust espresso that I poured into a big, American-sized cup, not realizing that it wasn't normal coffee.

I was way over-caffeinated on this very hot and humid morning as I waited outside for a bus. My heart began beating unevenly and then too quickly. By the time the bus had climbed the hill to the main square, I was sweating and hyperventilat-ing. I got off the bus and slumped on the steps of a one-star hotel, feeling as if I were going to pass out.

"Do you need help?" asked a young man in accented English. He helped me stand, and I leaned on him for sup-port as he took me to the *Ospedale*, the only hospital in Capri.

To say that this hospital was an *incubo*, nightmare, would be a gross understatement. An orderly wheeled me inside over a dirt floor and then over a wooden plank that covered the dirt floor. The doctors all stood around smoking and the one who came in to see me reeked of cigarettes, on his hands and clothing.

"Aren't you going to check my heart?" I asked him in insufficient Italian. By now I was crying.

He took out a dirty-looking stethoscope and listened to my chest. "One hundred twenty beats per minute," he said in Italian.

"That's not good!" I nearly screamed.

He left the room and returned quickly with a three-inch hypodermic needle. All I could think was that he hadn't sterilized it. Oh, my God, I was going to die in a filthy hospital on a beautiful island. "*No, non lo voglio!*" I cried. I don't want it!

Another doctor came in and spoke to me in English. She had kind eyes and gave me Valium. "Tell me, why are you here in Capri?" she asked.

"Dottoressa, I came alone for a weekend," I said. "I've been living in Rome for two years, alone."

"How do you like living in Italy?"

"I am trying so hard to make it work, but it has been very difficult," I said, still crying.

"I think you should consider going back home to the States where things are easier," she said. "I think it is maybe too stressful for you in this country."

My kind stranger, Salvatore, was still there, seated by my bed. He had stayed with me the entire time. When I was released, I was still shaky, and my throat felt tight, like I was being strangled. As he walked me to the bus to go back down the mountain to my hotel, he took my hand.

"You've been so kind to me. Thank you," I said.

"Can I take you to dinner tomorrow night?"

"Um, I'm not sure I'm up to it," I said. "Why don't you call first?"

I told the hotel that I was feeling ill and took a car service all the way back to Rome. It cost about $200, and I didn't even care. I just needed to get out of Capri, an island meant for lovers and couples and people who could tolerate excessive amounts of caffeine.

23

My meltdown in Capri scared me. It convinced me to take the summer off from my Rome adventure by staying in my old New York apartment, whose rent had so kindly been paid all this time by my mother and stepfather as a way of helping me out.

I hadn't given up on Italy. In fact, I had a new and quite different job lined up there that would start in October—teaching Jesuits how to speak English.

It wasn't the first time I had considered teaching English. Before I moved for the fifth time, I had become friendly with a lingerie shop owner who had wanted to hire me to teach her daughter conversational English. The daughter went back and forth, changing her mind several times, and in the end, decided to take the lessons with me. I had thought that if I got together a group of Italian clients, I'd be able to keep busy and make some money on the side.

Meanwhile, I had heard of this job teaching the Jesuits at Gregoriana University, whose campus of majestic white buildings was not too far from my apartment. The interviewer complimented my English and offered me the job, but there were two problems—only one of which I felt I could do something about.

The problem I could do something about was that I needed specific training in teaching ESL, English as a Second

Language. While I was in New York that summer, I took a class on it at the New School.

The problem I wasn't sure how to deal with was that the Jesuits were the most intelligent and educated Catholics in Rome, and the university was affiliated with the Vatican, no less. I knew I needed more training, and I got it at the New School, but I still doubted whether I'd be up to the challenge. I'd be teaching English at an intermediate level.

The more I read up on the Jesuits, the more fearful I became. I thought they would call me out as a fraud after only a single lesson.

I finished the New School course. I had my certification. I needed the money, and I needed the steadiness of a job I could depend on.

But I turned down the job.

The New School classes weren't a waste. I began to attract a following of people who wanted to learn conversational English. The shopkeeper's daughter was one of them. An Italian dubbing actress named Claudia was another. Soon I had a veritable little ESL salon going on in my apartment, where I charged students 50,000 *lire* per hour (about $30) to learn English from their very own American Myth. The group even included Alberto, the *grande bacciatore*, great kisser, who couldn't decide so long ago whether he wanted to make me his girlfriend.

I enjoyed teaching English and was a lot more confident in my skills as long as my students weren't steely-eyed Jesuits.

It was around this time that I finally received my long-awaited *permesso di lavoro*, the piece of paper that officially allowed me to work in the arts in Italy for a two-year period. I ran to the dubbing studio to give a big hug to Frank, my most ardent supporter in this nearly impossible quest for legitimacy.

I felt high on my accomplishment. I had been tenacious and done everything Italy had asked of me. I would not be defeated.

Oddly, now that I was making more of my living from teaching English, I received my first job offer to speak only in Italian. The wife of Nick Alexander, one of the dubbing directors, called me into the studio one day for an unexpected job. "It's a quick one-line job," she said.

"No problem."

"It's in Italian."

"Not in English?" I asked.

"You can do it," she assured me. "It's only one line and a bit of giggling for a movie called *Coconuts*, and we really need you right away."

My Italian really had improved immensely. I was working with a new teacher and, of course, speaking the language every single day for everything from shopping to dating. If my relationships with men were anything as improved as my language skills, I would have been quite happy.

My career (or, at least, my income) was on an upswing, and I was feeling more confident. This confidence must have radiated outward, just as my neediness advertised itself to potential suitors. A prominent casting director, Jeremy—a friend of my friend Derek—called me in to read for a part in an HBO film for television. It was called *Nicholas' Gift*, and I was only told that it was a good, though small, part.

I hated auditioning without preparation, not even knowing the role—but this was, after all, HBO.

"Great look," noted Jeremy when I got there. He handed me the script and gave me some time with it while he went inside to talk with the director.

The story was about a couple whose son gets shot during a robbery while they are traveling through Sicily. They donate the child's organs so that others may live. The role I was reading for was for someone named Loretta, the agent who rents the couple their car at the airport.

Ever since the Easter-candy episode, I'd been trying not to squint when I auditioned. Sometimes I slipped over into the opposite effect—eyes too wide and staring, like I was possessed. For this reading, the stakes were high—HBO!—so I was accordingly nervous. I went right into that familiar vicious cycle of anxiety that produced poor results that in turn increased my anxiety. When that happens, my performance goes to hell, and that was what happened now. I flubbed the first take, did worse on the second, and begged for a third, by which time I was a basket case.

"Do it again and watch the eyes," Jeremy cautioned.

After another take, he said, "Enough." My heart sank. I held my breath for the verdict.

"You're just what we're looking for," he said. "Come back this afternoon, and you'll read for the director."

I was walking on air. Actually, I was walking in puddles, because it rained steadily all day, but I was beyond excited. First, I spent time locating the address where the next reading would be held, so that I could find it easily later that afternoon. Then, I went home and blow-dried my hair again, since I was drenched from the rain.

At 5:30 I arrived at Banca dei Santo Spirito. I had worked myself into a state of nervous anticipation in which I was both afraid I would fail and also believed the role was mine, that mine that I was born to play a car-rental clerk. I had already promised to call my mother the minute I had any updates. "This could be it, Mom," I said. "The break I've been waiting for."

Jeremy was there with the director, a somber, bearded man. They only asked for one take, and I did the best I could. There's a disembodied feeling I get after I've read for someone. Jeremy gave me a reassuring wink, but I had no idea whether I'd bombed or aced it. I thanked them both for their time and went back into the rain.

By the next day, the anticipation was killing me. I called Jeremy on the pretext of thanking him again for the opportunity while really hoping for some feedback. "You were marvelous," he said, before lowering the boom. "He has his eye on someone else from the States, though. I think it's ridiculous, but that's it."

I thanked him again in a hollow voice and slithered low into my chair. At least he had called me "marvelous." I wasn't sure how far "marvelous" would take me, but it was something.

In my early days in Rome, the lack of a work permit was my biggest issue. Now that I had a permit, I knew it was all so much more complicated than that.

Yes, getting the permit had been a major accomplishment, but there was just not enough acting work to keep me busy. I started networking among friends, and friends of friends, which is how I met Francesco.

"You have a beautiful speaking voice," Francesco said. "Maybe I can help you."

Francesco, a friend of my friend Pier Paolo, spoke excellent English. He was cute, with long, dark-blond hair and a lovely, musical speaking voice of his own. That voice explained why he was an announcer for television specials, a dubbing actor, and also a jazz singer who specialized in Sinatra standards. He even sounded like Frank, but with an Italian accent.

Francesco was also one of those Italians with boundless energy, always commuting on his motorino all over Rome for his freelance jobs. He had a long-time girlfriend, Elizabetta, and so he became my newest guy friend—we'd have lunch once a week at a local restaurant called Tiepolo that reminded me of The Great American Health Bar where I had often lunched in Manhattan. We'd have baked potatoes stuffed with vegetables or tuna.

"I love your voice," he told me. "I will get you a voice job."

One place he often worked was at the Rai, and he was as good as his word—he immediately got me some work there reading copy in English. I didn't even have to audition.

24

In my New York summer, when I was learning how to teach ESL, I befriended a woman, Margaret, who was quite unhappy in her marriage and had no intention of rejoining her husband, Brian, back in Italy. Brian was a British diplomat on a two-year assignment in Rome. Margaret suggested I meet him in Rome for dinner and some company. The resulting dinner, at Mario dei Fiori, was not far from the Spanish Steps.

It was easy to talk to Brian, especially because we spoke only English the entire evening, a welcome relief, and even though he spent much of the time discussing his distress over Margaret leaving him. "I'm so sorry," I said as I touched his hand.

He took me home in a taxi. I sensed that if I asked him to come up, he would, but I played it cool and safe. He was boyishly cute, with straight blond hair and that gorgeous British accent, but he was clearly still in shock over the end of his marriage, and he was about to leave for Siena for a while to study Italian.

The following day I called to thank him for dinner. "We'll do it again when you're back from Siena," I said airily. It was always nice to have a new friend in Rome.

Wait, who was I kidding? I was already smitten. I couldn't help it. He was intelligent, he was interesting, and he had that cool diplomat job. I was even attracted to the idea that he, too, was needy. Finally, a man who might match me in the insecurity department! I went to bed that night with new hope and a smile.

I returned from the gym one late afternoon to find two phone messages from Brian. He was back from Siena and wanted to take me to dinner.

The next day he arrived at 5:00 p.m. while I was still taking my laundry out of the machine. "Want a hand hanging the sheets?" he asked, just like a real boyfriend.

We went upstairs to the rooftop terrace and hung sheets. It felt deliciously domestic. Was that all it took for me to fall for someone? I felt hopeful that Brian would be my new boyfriend, and also a little appalled at how easy it was for any man to grab my heart.

Back in my apartment, we talked so easily, for hours. When we got hungry, we went to a nearby restaurant for dinner. It was lovely, except for one thing—he kept circling back to Margaret. "I can't believe what she did to me," he mumbled into his food.

"I'm sorry," I repeated. I didn't tell him that I already knew from Margaret that she'd had an affair over the summer.

"We had already picked out our new home together. Now I'll have to live in it without her," he said. "Would you like to see it?"

"Sometime, sure," I said. I liked that this man was asking me back to his place, but I didn't like the idea that he was still thinking of it as "their" place.

When he walked me home, he asked if he could kiss me. After he kissed me, he apologized. "I'm in a very vulnerable place right now," he said.

"I understand."

Did I understand, really? I knew what people said—not to date men who were on the rebound, whether from wives or girlfriends. That they seemed passionate and available, but that it was smoke and mirrors. They were trying to blot out the memory of their ex, or get back at them, or drown their self-pity in someone who was new and handy. I wasn't the first woman who thought that maybe this time it would be different, that I could really be just what a man like Brian needed in his moment of pain and emptiness.

He invited me to dinner the next night at a place near the embassy where he worked. Afterward, he took me to see his temporary apartment where Margaret would have joined him. It was a shrine to her, full of photos of the two of them laughing it up in the sunshine of better days. There was even a photo of her in the bathroom.

"Brian," I said. "I really like you, but I need to know whether you're seeing me as a way to get back at Margaret, because that's not something I can do."

He seemed appalled. "I'm with you for *you*, Alison," he said. "I'm with you for *me*."

Well, that was all the proof I needed! He'd said the right words, and I believed him.

When he passed the Italian exam he needed for his diplomatic work, he took me out to celebrate at the renowned five-star Eden Hotel. I was wowed. That night we made love for the first time. He spent the entire night with me, and I loved having him in my bed, his arms wrapped around me. It felt so right. "I feel safe with you," he told me.

I liked that he felt safe with me, but I wasn't sure I felt safe with him, in the emotional sense. He still mentioned his ex far more often than necessary. He even invited a friend of his soon-to-be ex-mother-in-law, someone who knew Margaret well, to stay at his place when she came to town for a few days, which made me unaccountably jealous. I feared they would mostly be talking about Margaret and maybe even plotting to get Margaret back together with him. I was afraid he would never stop loving her. I spent that weekend alone. When it was over, he invited me to see the new house he'd be moving into, the one that he and Margaret had picked out together. It was near Villa Ada, a bucolic park. The house was gigantic—with five bedrooms and a large, modern kitchen. It had all new appliances and a washing machine. He had even ordered a clothes dryer. I had never met a single person in Rome who owned a dryer.

As we stood together on the large terrace with sweeping views of the mountains, Brian kissed me and held me close. "Will you be here to sit with me by the fireplace when it gets cold?" he asked. I swooned. Not a minute later he was talking about Margaret again.

"Do you wish it were her here with you instead of me?" I asked.

There are many ways he could have answered that question that would have sufficed. Instead, he chose to say, "I can't answer that."

In a movie version of my life, where I am a strong, sexy, confident heroine, I would walk out the door with my head held high, and my vision focused far ahead on a wonderful future. But this was not movie me. This was the real me: Alison who never gives up. Alison who looks for sunny resolutions to problems that cause her stomach aches. Most of my time with Brian was dream-like, and just the way I'd imagined it would be: cooking dinner together from fresh, simple Italian ingredients. Making love. Two in the tub, naked, by candlelight. Brian took an AIDS test without complaint, and everything was fine: the test was negative, our love was positive. But Brian was still Brian, and I was still me, and when I helped him pack to move into the five-bedroom house, I balked at having to help him carefully wrap frame after frame of blissful photos of him and Margaret and their adored cat.

"Careful with those," said Brian. "Could you put each one safely in between a few sweaters?"

I felt stabs of jealousy, as if his decision to take care of the photos meant he was practically cheating on me. I shopped with him as if we were a real couple, helping him pick out towels and linens for the new place, and when we lugged home the purchases, there was Margaret, staring at me out of picture frames everywhere, even on the kitchen counter. I hated Brian for putting me through this, and I hated myself for putting up with it, or for feeling anything about it at all. It took everything I had not to tell him that his wife had found someone new way before their marriage ended, that she had moved on, and that it was time for him to move on, too.

I had hoped that Brian would come to his senses on his own, but he didn't. "Are you planning to hang all those pictures of you and Margaret?" I finally asked him. "It hurts me."

Brian hung his head and began to cry. "I'm so sorry. I wasn't thinking," he said. "All of this represents my life with her, and it's painful, but Margaret represents my past. I think of you as my future."

Once again, he was easily able to win me over. The photos came down—or at least the one in the kitchen was gone the next time I came over.

In early December 1997, Brian and I spent a romantic weekend in Todi, in Umbria. We stayed at a *pensione* and took walks around the exquisite hill town, hand in hand, lingering in cafes over cappuccinos. I hadn't been so comfortable sleeping all night next to a man since my marriage more than ten years before.

Outside a twelfth-century church in the middle of the town square, we had some tourists take our picture together for the first time. Soon he'd be going back to England to spend the holidays with his family, and I'd be going back to the States to spend it with mine.

"I'm going to tell Margaret about us in the new year," he said.

Although Margaret had encouraged me to seek Brian out "for company," she still didn't know that we had started seeing each other romantically.

For Christmas, I gave Brian a beautiful, overpriced wool sweater in grey tones from upscale Bergdorf Goodman. He gave me a wool hat and gloves from London. "I missed you," he said.

"I missed you too. Did you tell Margaret?"

"She wasn't too happy about it. She said she was furious with you."

I'd been afraid that Margaret would suddenly want him back. She didn't. What finally broke us up was Brian's ex-boss, in a way.

When the ex-boss came to town, Brian had her stay with him, but would not invite me over for the entire time she was there. "She knew Margaret. It would be awkward," he said.

"What's awkward is that you keep me hidden from everyone else in your life," I said.

"I told Margaret, didn't I?"

"Yes, finally, but you don't invite me out with your friends or your business colleagues. You keep me like some kind of secret, as if ... as if I were your illicit lover. I thought I was special to you."

"Well..." he began. "I guess I'm not ready to introduce you. I don't feel like we're partners, in the end. It's really about sex, isn't it?"

Movie me would have told him off in a spectacular monologue that would leave the audience cheering for me. The real me, though, cried and acted hurt and stammered my way through the end of that telephone conversation, the last I would ever have with the diplomat who lacked the diplomacy to break up with me in person.

I was devastated. And angry. I was about as angry as I'd ever been—both with Brian and with myself.

I should have known better. After all this time in Italy, I should have learned something about relationships, and not just with Italian men. I should have learned something about myself.

I could not reconcile this war between my brain and my heart, so I gave up, and succumbed to yet another virulent strain of influenza. Fever, chills, vertigo.

I woke up on, of all days, Valentine's Day, lonely and miserable and aching inside and out, and decided in my feverish state that the only thing I could possibly do to make myself feel better was to try on the slinky new red Max Mara dress I had recently bought myself. It would make me feel sexy. I would feel beautiful and desirable again. I would no longer feel invisible. I stood on tiptoe on the blue loveseat to see myself completely in the full-length mirror. And the decision I'd struggled with back and forth for so long—whether to remain in Rome and make a go of it, or whether to crawl back to New York with my tail between my legs and admit that I'd failed—that decision was finally made for me.

I teetered on the blue love seat until I lost my balance. I fell and broke my back. My Roman adventure thus came to an abrupt halt—upended, toppled, broken, shattered into a million pieces.

PART 3

PART 3

25

I rested my gym bag on my lap as the crosstown bus made its fitful way across midtown Manhattan. Swimming laps for 20 minutes a day was about the best I could do, and pretty much the only thing I could manage.

The emergency room doctor in Rome had told me I'd fractured two vertebrae in my lower back, L1 and L3. There was no point to staying in Italy for a long recovery period when I had no real support system and at first could barely move my left leg more than a few inches. I gave up my apartment on Lungo Tevere Flaminio and returned to the Manhattan apartment my mother and George had kept going while I was away.

My orthopedist in New York said that swimming would be good for me. Every day, I took the crosstown bus to a place with a nice, clean pool on the East Side. I gingerly changed into my one-piece tank suit and did a sloppy doggy paddle for 20 minutes. Getting up the ladder from the pool and washing my hair and changing my clothing all took time because I moved slowly and cautiously. By the time I got home, I had barely enough energy to watch *Oprah* in bed.

I slowly improved, but my dizziness persisted. It was probably from banging my head on the steel radiator when I fell off the loveseat. I could barely stand without some wobble and probably looked to people in the street as if I were drunk.

On the advice of my orthopedist, I also saw a neurologist. My goal was just to have her clear me to work out in the gym again because at least a hit of endorphins would make me feel like I was on my way back to normal, but the neurologist told me to stick with swimming for now. "I think you have vertigo, and swimming may help control it," she said.

I tried not to think about what I had left behind, but I was plagued by all the what-if's: What if I hadn't fallen? Would I have been cast in a role by now in a Lina Wertmüller film? The Stallone movie had opened in the States just two months earlier, but I had no desire to see it. Someone I knew had seen it and said she had not seen me in any scene, anywhere. The movie had gotten poor reviews, and I had been left on the cutting-room floor even in a *lousy* movie.

What had I accomplished from almost three years of living abroad? What would I do now? I poked around inside myself, like testing a loose tooth, and found no desire, anywhere, to return to acting. All I wanted was to get my body back, to feel rooted and grounded in a life that was mine, whatever that life looked like. I wanted an end to the pain, and not just in a physical sense.

As my body began to get stronger, I resumed interest in having a social life. I signed up online for a dating site and turned from watching TV to going through hundreds of personals, trying to assess from the photos and the write-ups whether any of these men might be a match for me. None of them were going to admit in his ad that he had a fear of commitment or was a bad kisser, but then I wasn't going to admit that I was overly needy and that my penchant for romanticizing everything meant that I often didn't assess the situation clearly. I misread the signs and stuck with men who clearly weren't going to work out.

I combed through the ads very carefully, applying the same caution with which I now moved my legs. I finally started up an online flirtation with a cute guy who looked to be around my age. He had sparkling blue eyes and a quick wit. We began speaking by phone, and he exuded a vibrant personality. He said he was a social worker, which I found fascinating. I, too, loved the idea of helping people with whatever problems they presented, perhaps because I had always relied on others helping me through my own problems. He must be a good person to be a social worker, I assumed. He worked with people who had alcohol and drug issues.

John usually called by 8:00 p.m., so I always made sure I was home by then. We developed a long, fruitful phone friendship before I agreed to meet him in person.

He drove to the city from his home in upstate New York. He was even better looking than in his photos, which was unusual, with deep blue eyes and an electric smile.

After about four months of dating, we went on a weekend skiing trip upstate. I was now healed enough to ski, although I had at best been an intermediate skier and hadn't done it in years. I figured I would stick to the beginner slopes, at least until I was sure of what my body could handle.

Our first day on the slopes, John suggested we hit the Devil's Notch run.

"Um, that's a little advanced for me," I said.

"I thought you said your back was all healed? We'll do the lower part that's easier. Come on. I'll go down first and watch you. That way I can give you pointers."

If my back wasn't rigid and unyielding before, it certainly was now. I had wanted to ease into this, not qualify for the Olympics. Somehow, I managed to get down the easier part of that insane run.

John whizzed past me and met me at the bottom. "Wow, you're not as good as I thought," he said. "You definitely need lessons."

His eyes, which I had thought of as a laughing blue, were now a cold, icy blue. Why hadn't I noticed that earlier?

The one good thing I got from my relationship with John was the idea of trying my hand at social work. I had always loved the idea of being in a "helping" profession. I was a great listener, had empathy for others, and with my family background of loss and illness, I was able to connect with others who had been through similar experiences. I knew it wasn't a high-paying profession, but I had never been in any job or career for the money alone. I loved the idea of doing something rewarding and difficult, and to be able to help people who were struggling.

The only thing was that I would have to go back to school and get a master's degree for this kind of work. That worried me. I had always been told that I was the pretty one, not the smart one, and I had only finished two years of college before quitting to become a flight attendant. That meant I had to finish my undergraduate degree and *then* get a master's. What if I wasn't good enough to get into *any* college, or to even get a bachelor's degree?

I searched for a university with a good social-work program where I could get both degrees. Fordham seemed like a good fit and was located within walking distance of my apartment. There I could get a liberal arts undergraduate degree with a minor in social work, and then continue on to the master's ... *if* I could get in at all.

When I took the required entrance exam, guess what? I was nervous! Some things never change. But the next day they called to say I had passed. I was in.

Did that calm my nervousness? No! Now I was as terrified of academia as I'd been of the idea of teaching the Jesuits. However, my unwillingness to give up kicked in, the one thing I could count on to balance out the anxieties that wanted to keep me in bed, watching TV. I forged ahead, thinking of my future practice where I would be able to help people, make an impact on their lives. This was to be my new passion.

First, I had to swallow my pride. For many years I had tried to steer conversations away from how I had never graduated college. I didn't mind telling them I'd gone to Dalton, the elite Upper East Side high school, but when the conversation turned to college I'd become vague. When did I graduate? I'd mumble the year I *would* have graduated, had I done so. If they persisted in asking about my college experience, I would pivot and counter with something totally off-topic, like, "Have you traveled a lot?" I was embarrassed about my academic past. It was proof, I thought, that maybe I was a failure, or not intelligent enough, or that I was not a serious person or a person to be taken seriously. Everyone else I knew had a college degree. Now I had to keep a low profile alongside all the younger students. I was 39 years old, and they were half my age.

I entered a program that would allow me to graduate with a baccalaureate in social work and took one year off the two-year master's program, but I still had many compulsory undergraduate classes to finish before I could get the higher degree.

I studied constantly—every night, every afternoon. Weekends, too. I let go of plans with friends and only allowed myself one night a week to go out. School became my life. I took it more seriously than any job I had ever held. I needed to prove to myself that I could do this—that I could change course in all ways, no matter my age, and achieve a new goal.

I got straight A's in every subject.

For the first time, I was not focused on men, only on studying. Naturally, as soon as I did not focus on men, one crept into my life—an architect named Michael. We began as friends, but soon became intimate. He was from both an Italian and Irish background—slightly balding, with a strong nose and friendly hazel eyes. He had a wry sense of humor and the ability to make me laugh until it hurt. It had been forever since a man was able to make me laugh like that.

I felt a certain stability with Michael. It was time to move forward and get a puppy.

Michael and I took a drive to Saugerties, in upstate New York, to meet Sharon, a poodle breeder that the American Kennel Club highly recommended. Before we even rang the doorbell, we heard the deafening barking of Sharon's 12 poodles. Sharon, with curly, short hair, herself looked a bit like a 13th poodle.

There was only one female in the bunch, "The last female puppy for the season," said Sharon. It was a small, chocolate mini-puppy, three months old and slightly aloof. She didn't want to come over to check me out, and I worried whether she would ever warm up to me.

Nevertheless, I took her home and named her Alba, meaning the dawn, or sunrise, in Italian. I felt like Michael and I were a family.

Of course, I had no idea how to train a puppy. She wasn't cuddling on my lap the way I had envisioned. I was afraid that she didn't like me.

Michael offered to take Alba half the week to help with the training. It was like having shared custody. One day I went over there to visit them both, and Alba scrabbled across the floor to greet me and jumped into my arms, tail wagging away.

From that point on, I was in love with Alba. She stayed with me full-time, and I couldn't even write my school papers without her under my desk or near my feet. I liked Michael just fine, but Alba and I were inseparable.

26

T hings were going well. And then, one morning, I woke up with burning pain all down the front of my body. It happened suddenly, and it frightened me. "You need to have a brain MRI," my neurologist told me, which certainly did not make me feel any better. All I could think about was that I had to finish school. The pain erupted on a Monday, and that night I went to class anyway, my eyes puffy and my body on fire from my face to my feet.

The neurologist ordered a series of tests to try and determine what was going on with my body. Nothing showed up on these tests, except for one that measured the nerve pulses from the brain to the cervical spine, the neck. It was an uncomfortable test that involved electrodes and some guy pressing a button on a machine that made me jump and twitch from electrical shocks. I felt like I was in a torture chamber.

"The results show that something is abnormal, but we don't know what, or why," said the neurologist.

Again, not very comforting. "Abnormal?" I fairly screeched. Did that mean that *I* was abnormal, something I had always feared? Why couldn't I have a nice, simple diagnosis, like shingles? Why did I have to be the one about whom the best that could be said was that my nerves were abnormal?

Of all my numerous blood tests, only one—for an autoimmune illness—was slightly elevated, but this was inconclusive.

It could mean that my nerves were attacking my nerves. Or it could mean nothing. All that was certain was that I felt an unrelenting burning and stinging over the front of my body, right up into my face.

It didn't seem fair. I had tried to create a new life in Italy for three years. Now I was trying another new life, and it was just one setback after another.

Nevertheless, I continued through school that year, despite the pain. I didn't miss a single class. When my body went into flare-up mode, which it did at will, I would hurry home after class and curl up in bed with Alba, but I was scared.

I went to another neurologist for a second opinion. "We'll need to take a lot of tests to make sure you're not crazy," he said.

Crazy? Was that my real diagnosis? Was that what had been holding me back all these years, all my life?

But of course, I was not crazy. Maybe sensitive, but not crazy. Even the doctor had to admit it after running the same tests as the first neurologist and getting the same results: Something was definitely wrong, but he didn't know what, and he didn't know why.

All I knew was that I had to finish school. I was still dating the architect—and he insisted on coming to every doctor visit with me—but the idea of finishing school was what drove me. I needed to establish myself in a meaningful career. I kept telling myself that the pain would disappear one day, as suddenly as it had appeared. Meanwhile, I would just tough it out and go to school and continue to get all A's.

I wasn't crazy, but as anyone who lives with chronic pain and an uncertain diagnosis can tell you, it's easy to become crazy if you live with this long enough. Even when the pain felt like a 10, I'd underestimate it as a 9 because I couldn't allow the pain to run my life. Even as it created more and more of a divide between my real, pain-filled world and my fantasy world in which I attended my classes and worked toward my fantasy goal of having any kind of career, when no kind of career was going to work if this pain kept up. The neurologist suggested infusions of gamma globulin, a human plasma, but I was scared of the possible repercussions and turned it down. "Perhaps now would be a good time to speak with an immunologist?" she asked again when the pain hadn't subsided.

The immunologist also recommended infusions of gamma globulin. I agreed to try it out of desperation. It required that I sit for four hours in the treatment room, at the end of which I felt no diminution in pain, but had a big new problem: a headache so severe that the neurologist called it a meningeal-type headache. The pain stayed the same, but the headache was the gift that kept on giving—for a full week. No more infusions after that.

I tried various medications, but I couldn't tolerate the side effects of most of them. I tried an older tricyclic antidepressant called Elavil, but it gave me brain fog, as if I were living inside a big marshmallow. It also gave me dry-mouth and made me sleepy. Ultram made me nauseated. Opioids made me dizzy.

I was referred to a third neurologist, who said he had treated many patients for similar nerve pain. In fact, he had experienced the same kind of pain himself, a burning nerve pain with no clear diagnosis. "I couldn't even put socks on. Too much pain," he told me.

At least this doctor knew for sure that I wasn't crazy. After carefully going over the list of the medications I had already tried, he suggested methadone.

"Oh my God, that's for drug addicts!" I said.

"We also use it to treat severe nerve pain. We find it can really help," he said. "I'll start you on a very low dose, and we can always increase it."

I took the pill. It kept me up all night with my heart hammering inside my chest. There was no "high" feeling, just an anxiety so severe that the night felt endless. The neurologist stopped that treatment immediately.

I was ultimately given gabapentin, an anti-seizure pill. It caused fatigue and short-term memory lapses, but it also lessened the nerve pain just a little, and that was something. He also gave me my first official diagnosis: "idiopathic small fiber sensory neuritis," SFSN. I was grateful just to know what to call it.

"You'll see, the pain will burn itself out," he promised.

It never did.

I got my master's degree anyway. After seven years of going back to school part-time, including two field-placement internships that were required as part of the master's program; I finally completed my baccalaureate in social work followed by my master's in social work. I graduated summa cum laude.

It was my greatest achievement, but what made it all so special and worthwhile was having David come to my graduation ceremony. Having my beloved brother come with me was like having a father proudly giving his daughter's hand in marriage. David had been more of a father to me than my own dad, and seeing his pride in my accomplishments swelled me with my own sense of pride. The degree itself was a piece of paper, but David witnessing me getting this degree was the ultimate joy. He had always believed in me, and I had not let him down.

David had planned on coming up for my graduation for a year. He took an overnight train from Florida. I was so happy to see him, but I was aghast at how bad he looked. I knew that the train ride was an ordeal for him, with his Crohn's disease, but I wasn't prepared for how thin and worn he looked. I felt selfish for even agreeing to let him come.

Alba revived him on the couch with slurpy kisses and non-stop tail wags that moved like a fast drum roll. Alba, with her doggie sense of when someone was not well, stayed by David's side, with one paw placed comfortingly on his lap.

"Are you sure you're okay?" I asked him.

"I wouldn't miss this for the world, little one," he assured me, and immediately turned the spotlight back on me. That's how generous he always was, but I certainly wasn't going to admit I had terrible nerve pain that day. My suffering was nothing compared to what he was going through, and what he'd been going through for years. Nevertheless, I knew from the intent look of his beautiful, loving, blue-grey eyes that he could see I was in pain. No one in the world understood chronic pain better than he.

My neuritis did not go away. I never knew when to expect a flare-up. Some days I felt pretty good, and on others, I would wake up with a stinging pain along the tops of my feet and the shin area, a precursor of a full-body flare-up that could last weeks or even months. On a bad day, I would take multiple gabapentin capsules and curl up in a ball with Alba.

No doctor was able to take the pain away completely. There was no known cure.

I hid behind an occasional smile that masked my despair. I felt like my personality had changed since my time in Rome, where I was at least relatively energetic—going to dinners and parties, going out on jobs, dealing with all of Italy's bureaucracies and craziness. All I had needed was an afternoon nap, and I was good to go. Now my entire social life revolved around flare-ups of my nerve pain. I still went to the gym, even when I had stinging pain, and I toughed it out as best I could, it was the hibernation at home that I most looked forward to, curling up with Alba. My timidly hopeful mantra each night was, "In the morning it will be better."

I had to face it: I would not be able to take a full-time job in social work, not while I was in this condition. I didn't have the energy it required. After all this time and effort, after seven years of school and training, the best I could hope for was part-time work, and there wasn't much of that available.

In some ways, I was more isolated than I'd ever been. I looked fine on the outside, so friends must have wondered why I canceled plans so suddenly due to flare-ups of the nerve pain. I was with the architect for several years, but the relationship ultimately wasn't able to survive the stresses of my course load and near-constant pain, and that he always seemed to have one foot out the door.

In other ways, I did not feel so isolated after all. I remained on friendly terms with the architect, even after the breakup. I had stayed true to my academic and career goals, and felt accomplished and proud of myself, even though I worried about how I'd be able to hold down a full-time job if this chronic pain continued. Instead of focusing on who was here or not here for me, I had come through for *myself*, and it felt good.

27

My sister and I shared our deep concern for our brother, if little else. We spoke more often as David's health deteriorated over the next few years.

"Have you spoken with him?" she'd ask.

"Yes," I'd respond. "He doesn't sound good."

That's how our conversations went—always worried for him, always feeling helpless about it. David had infections deep inside his body and was always in and out of doctors' offices and hospitals. I spoke with him every day, and usually he'd sound peppier by the end of the call.

But not this time.

"You sound awful," I blurted out in spite of myself. "Please, tell me what I can do for you?"

He was silent for a moment, which already scared me.

"I'm not doing well," he admitted. "One of these days, and maybe soon, I'm going to die."

"No! Don't talk that way," I said. "I know you're feeling down right now, but—"

"You asked if there was something you could do for me, and there is," he said, interrupting me. "I need you to prepare for this. When the time comes, and it will, I'm going to need you to let go of me."

"No, David, please, you can't leave me!" I sobbed. I knew it was selfish of me, but I couldn't bear the thought of living in a world that didn't contain my sensational older brother, my forever rock.

"Listen, Alison. I have sepsis from all these infections. It's in my blood. I have to deal with it, and you're going to have to deal with it, too."

"Don't say this. Maybe you'll get better," I pleaded. "Please, you can't leave me."

I loved David so much. I felt I would do anything for him, anything at all. Except this, the one and only thing he was asking of me. I could not accept that he was dying, or that he would ever die. For years I had prevented myself from thinking about it or acknowledging how sick he was. Denial was a wonderful, terrible thing. It allowed me to live without the pain of knowledge, but it took an immense amount of physical and emotional effort to keep that masquerade going for myself.

Soon after that shocking conversation, David miraculously began to feel a little better. He had tried another medication, and his infections were slightly less painful, his voice more upbeat. I scurried right back into my world of denial.

I still had my brother. Everything was going to be okay.

"Little one, maybe we can go away together somewhere for a week," he said. "A little vacation, just you and me."

"I'd love that!" I said. "I'll go wherever you want!"

"How about a cruise to one of those islands in the Caribbean? They leave from Florida all the time."

We planned to do it in May. One afternoon in March, he called from the cell phone that he rarely used.

"Little one," he said, his voice sounding strangled, "I've had an accident." He had fallen down while waiting to see his doctor and was unable to stand up afterward.

"What do you mean?" I said.

"My foot fell asleep, and I couldn't support myself, so I fell over on my side. I just went down. And then I couldn't get up."

The medications David had taken most of his life had made his bones brittle. A fall like that was a terrible blow. As sick as he'd been, David had always been relatively independent, but now he was confined to a bed in the ER and wasn't sure when he'd be able to leave, and whether it would be under his own steam or in a wheelchair.

It happened that March 17 when David called me was the same date on which our father had died of a heart attack many years before. The significance of the date did not escape him. "Maybe it's a sign," he said.

Within a few hours, he told me the result of his x-rays: his hip was broken. "That's it for me," he said. No amount of arguing with him or consoling him could make him feel better.

After a week in the hospital, they took him by ambulance to another hospital where a skilled surgeon would try to set the broken bone in place by stretching out the leg so that the hip bone could fuse, using pins, screws, and rods. Surgery was out of the question because of David's infections, so this was the only option.

I flew down to Florida to see him right after the procedure. I brought him sweatpants and a sweatshirt to easily get in and out of, plus toiletries and other helpful items—plus cigarettes. A lifelong smoker, he'd be able to enjoy those from his wheelchair outdoors in between sessions at rehab. I couldn't bring a gin-and-tonic into his hospital room, so the cigarettes would have to do.

David was clearly in pain, but he remained upbeat at least for the few days I was down there. He announced that he was determined to walk again, and I believed him. But when I got back to New York, I fell into the shadows of fear. What if he was never able to walk again? What if he never recovered?

After the surgeon removed the pins and screws, he pronounced the hip strong enough that David was moved to a rehab facility. Three months later—right before his birthday in June—he was allowed to go home, although he needed a nurse's aide to help him a few times a week, along with visits from a physical therapist. He still had intense pain, despite all the meds he was taking, but in between watching hockey's Stanley Cup playoffs, he was able to walk somewhat on his own. I would have considered all this a move in the right direction, except that he no longer had any appetite, not even for hamburgers, and even the mention of a gin and tonic couldn't bring back the glimmer in his eyes.

I called my mother on her 88th birthday—she lived alone now that George had died a few years before, and although she had moderate dementia she was still able to live independently. After the call, I went to the Metropolitan Museum to see an exhibit on the Impressionists.

When I got home, I saw that my sister had called from her alternate phone, but she hadn't left a message. I dialed the number, and my brother-in-law answered.

"Did Deane call me?" I asked.

"I don't know how to tell you this so I'll just ... Your brother died," he said. "I'm sorry."

Somehow, despite all the evidence, I had thought that David would get better and that we would take that cruise to the Caribbean, even if I had to push his wheelchair along the deck. By protecting myself from the knowledge that he was going to die, I was left utterly unprotected at that moment when knowledge forced its way in, tearing down all the walls I had so carefully built ever since David developed this disease as a child. It was almost an out-of-body experience, this trauma, this utter shock.

Dead? My David, my brother, my lifelong best friend ... dead?

After our childhood separation, my sister and I had never been close. But the first thing I did was to call her. "We need to be together," I said.

Deane and I coordinated on how to help our mother deal with David's death, and how to mourn as a family. We went down to Florida, where Deane and her husband cleaned out and closed up David's house, and I stayed with Mom as she wavered between fully comprehending and barely comprehending what had happened.

When I saw my mother, I broke into tears. She was frail and so much thinner than last I saw her, even though it hadn't been very long. I knew it didn't help for me to be so upset when so much was going on, but I didn't know how to handle the onslaught of despair, and the fear of my own essential loneliness, now unleavened by David's constant presence in my life.

People called. People came by. It was all a blur. When my father's first cousin, Grace, called from Virginia and asked to speak with me after she was on the phone for a while with my sister, I didn't want to talk. I barely remembered Grace from last I'd seen her thirty years ago. I took the call only because to do otherwise would be rude.

"How are you holding up, Alison?" she asked.

"Not too well," I said, my voice trembling. "I can't stand the pain."

"I understand."

Thank God Grace didn't offer some of the platitudes people were saying, that it was a blessing David was no longer suffering.

"I really don't feel much like talking," I said.

"I know," said Grace. "May I call you when you're back in New York?"

I said yes just to be polite.

Once I returned from Florida, I still didn't want to talk to anyone. I lay on my bed with Alba, with the TV on for the distraction of white noise, and my eyes shut tight. If it weren't for having to walk Alba, I wouldn't have left the house for weeks.

I can't say what the lowest point was. It was all one, long low point. And then someone called.

It was Grace.

She had a voice as light as air, like someone decades younger than her late eighties. Her voice had a singsong quality, like birds chirping. She was the rare person who was able to be upbeat and happy, even in the face of great loss.

Grace allowed me to fall apart on the phone as I grieved my brother. She listened tirelessly. She "got" me. "I understand. I know how you feel," she said over and over, and I believed her. She comprehended my grief and my fear.

She knew that I'd been closest of all to my brother, and that his loss felt fundamental to my very existence. She didn't tell me it was going to get better within any particular timeframe. She just allowed me to wail.

"Would you like it if I called you again in a few days?" she asked at the end of our one-sided conversation. I couldn't wait.

Grace called me every other day. It was the one thing I looked forward to.

She also emailed me funny photos of animals or witty, pithy sayings. She loved to talk about politics and her belief in social change. She always had CSPAN blasting in the background. She even went to sleep with the radio tuned to the news.

She told me about her life and her family and her hopes for the world. I told her more banal stuff, about my dates and my job search. She encouraged me in everything. "Things will get better," she always assured me in her melodic voice.

On a day after spring had supposedly arrived, she sent me a photo of a statue of a Greyhound dog on her snow-covered doorstep. She had wrapped the statue in a hat and scarf. The caption said, "Just don't know what to wear today."

Or other times I would send her a picture of Alba after she'd been groomed, with a note she'd supposedly typed out herself, and Grace would write back: "Lookin' good, Alba! No. 1 dog, and Olympic gold medal for Best Looking!"

It took a few months after David died before I began to date again. I didn't have my old energy, and I was still grieving for David, but I made an effort and went out with a few nondescript men I met through Match.com. Knowing I could fill Grace in on these dates made even the most boring ones bearable.

"How was the physicist?" she might ask.

"Consumed with his ex-wife," I told her. "Then he told me the list of other match.com dates he had lined up after me."

Grace laughed her infectious laugh. "Oh, that's hilarious," she said. "He's sharing with you!"

Then I would laugh, too. Grace made me see the humor in situations I had always regarded with melancholy. She was always able to lighten my mood.

"How was the professor?" she asked another time.

"I asked him why he moved to New York from Wisconsin, and suddenly he said his phone was vibrating, and he walked outside to take the call, and he never came back. I was left at the table sipping my wine for half an hour before the waiter told me he was gone."

"Oh, my!"

"He told me he was tenured, but I Googled him when I got home, and it turned out he'd been fired for hitting a student!"

"No wonder he had to leave in a hurry," said Grace. "He thought you were wearing a wire!"

Grace was always there for me. I tried to be there for her, too. I called her on the anniversary of the death of her beloved dog. "I know that today is rough," I said.

"I released a bunch of balloons up into the sky, and it made me feel better. And now, hearing your voice ... the day will be okay."

On a particularly frigid winter day she was late picking up the phone, and out of breath. "Sorry, I was outside feeding the birds. I don't know why they're still here so late in the season, but they deserve a nice breakfast like anyone else!"

"That's so sweet that you leave them food," I said.

"But they are so generous with gifts of their own," she said. "They sing, and they chirp for me. They give me the gift of happiness."

A week later I asked her how the birds were doing.

"Their nest is empty," she said. "They're gone."

"Oh, I'm sorry. I know you'll miss them. Are you sad?"

"I'm not sad at all!" said Grace. "They flew away, sure, but I still hear their songs."

A year after David died, my mother's breast cancer spread to her bones. She died six months later.

"One thing I know is that you made your mother very, very happy," Grace wrote to me in a note. "She was so proud of everything you did for her and had great confidence in you. She knew you would struggle with sadness, but she believed that you'd be all right because you're that kind of person. Everyone who loves you knows that about you."

28

It was hard to find a part-time job in social work, on top of which I faced a Catch-22: I needed certain experience to give me the qualifications for these jobs, but I couldn't get that experience until I actually *got* one of these jobs. I kept trying, but it was frustrating. I really needed something in Manhattan, but those went fast if they came up at all. Jobs in the outer boroughs would be a taxing commute.

I had finally gotten a job interview at the same time that my mother was dying. It was for part-time work at a hospital. Grace urged me to take the interview with the associate director of patient-care services despite the circumstances, and to follow up with the second interview after I got back from Florida.

"I'm not sure I can handle it," I said tearfully.

"Of course you can!" said Grace. "This job is perfect for you. Sure, the timing is not to be believed, but you'll be great. I have no doubt."

Grace was a glass-half-full person. My glass was always empty. The amazing thing was that Grace's glass always had enough, even as she poured extra into mine. She was steady and solid in her support, never wavering, never drawing back. Slowly, I felt that she was fiddling with my DNA, sprucing up my chromosomes.

Grace was filling me with life.

She was right: I could handle it. I got the job.

I was excited to have gotten my first social-work job and in a hospital setting. I loved learning about various illnesses, and speaking with doctors about the patients, and then showering the patients with warmth and empathy while trying to help them. But that wasn't what the job was like all the time. It wasn't even what the job was like most of the time.

Instead, it was mostly about processing new patients every day, and rarely being able to follow up with the ones I had met the day before. It was about doing paperwork and filing the proper documentation. It was fast-paced, requiring me to work quickly, instead of how I'd imagined it would be, where I would get to know individuals over time, really get into helping them sort through their problems. Patients were pushed along a fast-moving assembly line on their way to being discharged or to rehab units, where I would never encounter them again. The job was stressful and not right for me. I couldn't see it ever leading to the kind of one-on-one practice I'd had in mind. I wasn't great with computers, and a large part of my day had to do with entering and coding information in programs that stymied me.

I would have stuck with it anyway, for the tiny paycheck, the soupçon of self-esteem, but something happened. My dog, Alba, had not been well. She was exhibiting "fly-biting behavior," snapping at imaginary flies in the air. While it wasn't life-threatening, it was alarming. She needed medicine eight specific times each day to help control the fly-biting along with her other symptoms, including intermittent vomiting from a gastrointestinal disorder.

I know that people often have to contend with things like this—children, spouses, and pets who need them—and they don't always quit their jobs over it. However, I felt oppressed over having lost both my brother and my mother in a short span of time. I couldn't lose my dog, too; at least, I couldn't live with myself if I held onto a low-paying, unsatisfying job and it later turned out that this was my very last time to be together with Alba.

I made the right decision. Alba continued to get worse, with various underlying conditions fighting against each other. I brought her into the animal hospital after an episode that left her paralyzed. "She is suffering," the doctor told me.

I couldn't stand to lose her, but I couldn't stand to hear those words, either. My responsibility to Alba, as her friend, companion, and mommy, was to do what was right for her and to lessen her suffering. Agreeing to "put her down" would, of course, increase *my* suffering, but I couldn't look into her trusting brown eyes and deny her what she needed and deserved: to be at peace.

It happened on a February day when there was a blizzard. The sharpness and misery of the icy air reflected how I felt. My partnership with Alba had been the most intense and rewarding I'd ever had, far more so than with any boyfriend or with my ex-husband. Pet lovers know this, that the bond with a pet can easily rival that with another human being in terms of comfort and companionship.

I barely remembered my own address to give to the cab driver. When I got home, all I could see were reminders of Alba: the blue-doughnut bed she slept in when she wasn't curled up next to me. The torn stuffed pink elephant that she liked to play with.

Her chew toys. Her food bowl. "Is there nothing more we can do?" I had pleaded with the vet. "Anything?" But it would have been unthinkable to let Alba hang on for my sake. I had to let her go for hers.

I placed her leash on the bed next to me.

I told myself I would never get another dog. The pain of losing another dog someday was too great a risk. I would never take such a risk again. I would spend the rest of my life alone, if I had to.

"No one spends life alone," said Grace, who called me every single day after Alba died. As if to prove it, she alternated Thanksgivings between her family in Virginia, and visiting me in New York. I was welcome at those Virginia Thanksgivings, too, along with her grown son and two daughters. The last Thanksgiving she spent in New York was right before she turned 90—still with the musical voice of a 35-year-old.

Four months later, she died. Her son, Steve, called to break the news to me. I had just spoken to Grace a few days before, and she had been as upbeat and lively as ever. I had told her about my latest horrible match.com date, and she had said, "Try the next one. Call me later and report back."

Dear, sweet Grace. If you are listening—and I know you were *always* listening—I'm here to report that despite the incredible sadness I felt, and the terrible sense of loss, the next day after I heard from your son, I went back to the gym. I know you'll understand. That's what you always said: "I understand." You listened to me like I mattered, and everything you ever said matters to me, too.

You will be happy to know that I got another dog, Dea. I couldn't have opened my heart like this without you showing me the way.

Thanks to you, every time I go to the window I hear birdsong, even in winter. You sang this song of life to me, and now I sing it back to you.

ABOUT THE AUTHOR

Alison was born and raised in Manhattan where she currently lives. She is a licensed Master of Social Work, and while not working in the field at the moment, continues to take continuing education classes to keep up.

She has been an actress, mostly in commercials, and an advertising copywriter.

Alison is an avid dog person and plans for her dog to become a therapy animal to those in need.

In her spare time, she continues to take Italian classes in hope of becoming more proficient. She is also an exercise enthusiast, especially hiking and skiing.

This is her first book.

ACKNOWLEDGEMENTS

I wish to thank Devan Sipher for his helpful memoir writing class that crystalized my goal for writing this book and for his recommendation to meet with Jami Bernard. Without Jami's intellect, teaching skills, patience, and tough love this book would never have been written.

I also say thank you to my friend, Riccardo Mei, who many years ago egged me on to write about my experiences and life in Italy. I say thank you to Bill Adler for his support along the way, and to Daniel Stashower for his help and generosity. I also thank my friends who always told me that I could do this. But most of all, I thank Grace because she was the first person to read something that I wrote and always told me I could do it.